Officially Withdrawn

The Horizons of the Flesh

CRITICAL PERSPECTIVES ON
THE THOUGHT OF MERLEAU-PONTY

Edited by

Garth Gillan

SOUTHERN ILLINOIS UNIVERSITY PRESS
Carbondale and Edwardsville

Feffer & Simons, Inc.
London and Amsterdam

Library of Congress Cataloging in Publication Data

Gillan, Garth, 1939–
  The horizons of the flesh.

  Includes bibliographical references.
  1. Merleau-Ponty, Maurice, 1908–1961. I. Title.
B2430.M38G55   194   73–3154
ISBN 0–8093–0605–0

Copyright © 1973 by Southern Illinois University Press
All rights reserved

Printed in the United States of America
Designed by Gary Gore

929823

CONTENTS

PREFACE

ALTHOUGH spread out among the various studies comprising this volume, there is one intention animating this collection: to bring to expression the levels and directions through which the thought of Merleau-Ponty moved from *The Structure of Behavior*[1] to *The Visible and the Invisible*.[2] There is a central question dominating Merleau-Ponty's works only if its discovery follows the path of the interpretation of myth outlined by Levi-Strauss in *The Raw and the Cooked*, which moves "not along a linear axis but in a spiral."[3] If it is possible to start with the perceptual meaning of behavior as does *The Structure of Behavior* and with perception as a meaningful behavior, then it is also imperative to explore the world that perceptual behavior opens onto and the corporeal subjectivity that is that world. Thus one comes to the *Phenomenology of Perception*.[4] But at the same time one comes to *Humanism and Terror*[5] and to *Sense and Non-Sense*,[6] for the world onto which perception opens is created through expression and through the attempts of men to come to terms with their own history. Politics finds its point of intelligibility in an ontology that begins with the fundamental need to understand the necessity and freedom interwoven in the circumstances of human action. The *Adventures of the Dialectic*[7] stands in that same line of questioning, for the categories in which we express the world we see and touch cannot be other than those in terms of which we act and intervene in the history of that visible world.

Signs,[8] "The Eye and the Mind,"[9] and *The Visible and the Invisible* are the culmination, in point of time, if certainly not in intention, of that search for the bases in language and perception, art and politics—the dimensions of expression—through which to express and experience the sense and nonsense of the human world.

For in the "existential eternity" of the *flesh,* the element of being which emerges from the pages of those works, Merleau-Ponty confronts the founding dimension of the pact of men with the world upon which all action and expression depend and in terms of which they find their most comprehensive intelligibility. The passage to the ontology of the flesh is not a labyrinth; it is, to pick up on the expression borrowed from Levi-Strauss, a spiral. It is an allusive and indirect passage; there are no theses, only the texture of a thought woven from the dense strands of the body which bind man to the world. The thought that inhabits those works is not a statement of an opinion upon the nature of the world, but the construction of the framework in which to speak the world and in which to make the world speak.

To that end it is necessary to examine what has not been examined before and to bring together themes and ideas which, at first glance, seem to be foreign to each other. From that perspective, we arrive at the title and intention of this collection: to bring into relief the interlocking questions which form the texture of the thought of Merleau-Ponty. From the reading of the works of Merleau-Ponty which the studies included in this volume establish, it becomes clear that the unity of Merleau-Ponty's thought lies within the very demands that language places upon expression. For Merleau-Ponty's development from *The Structure of Behavior* to *The Visible and the Invisible* calls into question the very nature of philosophical reflection and the interpretation of the sciences. What is it to speak the world, to bring to expression within language the truth of the world? That question haunts the pages of Merleau-Ponty's works. What is at stake is not the methodology of a distinct and separate discipline which can take its place alongside the distinct methodologies of the human and exact sciences, but, as was the case for Husserl in *The Crisis of European Sciences and Transcendental Phenomenology,* what is at stake is the very understanding of rationality and the fate of reason in history.

Each study follows the course of that contested rationality by exposing its consequences in one side or another of Merleau-Ponty's thought. It is necessary, first of all, to establish the contours of the reading of Merleau-Ponty's works—something to which great care has not been given in the past. But, at the same time, interpretation is necessary in order for that reading to take on the trenchant character of philosophical responsibility. From the beginning the thought of Merleau-Ponty has been burdened with the title "philosophy of ambiguity." But it is essential to see that ambiguity and the recognition of contingency in being and in history which that title implies are not ways to resolve the problems that the world of the body and history pose for expression, but ways to provide the framework in which the relevant questions can be raised. In a sense, the ambiguity of the world of the body radically prohibits thought from taking a position, if to take a position vis-à-vis the world is to force the issue of truth. Merleau-Ponty's thought must be viewed as a discourse at once descriptive and reflective: its intention is to disclose the strangeness of the world, but to do so in accord with the structure of significance in language—through detours and divergences.

What is common to each study in this collection, then, is a simple aim: to unfold the text and in unfolding the text to expose the rapport of the text with the world signified in its language. The touchstone of interpretation is that rapport. For the texts of an author reveal a common world, shared by all. Yet they weigh that world down with their own significations, and, in doing so, they literally chart a course along whose markings we can follow with our own eyes the contours of its shape. It is that type of interpretation that is valuable in the studies forming this collection. To the conception of the thetic nature of thought there corresponds the conception of interpretation as judgment and assessment. But judgment on the basis of what, and assessment in terms of what world and what truth? The answer to that question has already been given: on the basis of the world common to all which each text of Merleau-Ponty unfolds in the contrasts and oppositions forming its language. And placed within that world, our concern is to learn to see and to speak. That is to take a position in the true sense: to recognize the heights and depths, the shadows and clearings of the world and thus discover in what direction we must walk. To that end we find, in the languages of perception, science, art, and politics, signs which point the way.

I wish to thank the publishers for permission to use quotations from *The Phenomenology of Perception* by Maurice Merleau-Ponty,

New York: Humanities Press, Inc., 1962, and Routledge & Kegan
Paul Ltd., 1962.

GARTH JACKSON GILLAN

Carbondale, Illinois
September 1972

NOTES ON CONTRIBUTORS

GARTH GILLAN, Associate Professor of Philosophy at Southern Illinois University, is a graduate of Duquesne University. He is the author of articles on the phenomenology of language and semiotics and is currently working on a study of critical semiotics and, with Alphonso Lingis, on a translation of the works of Emmanuel Levinas.

DON IHDE is Professor of Philosophy at the State University of New York at Stony Brook. He is the author of *Hermeneutic Phenomenology: The Philosophy of Paul Ricoeur* and of numerous articles on auditory experience and the phenomenology of language. Currently he is working on a study of man and technology.

ALPHONSO LINGIS, Associate Professor, The Pennsylvania State University, is the translator of Merleau-Ponty's *The Visible and the Invisible* and Emmanuel Levinas's *Totality and Infinity*. He has written many articles on various figures and aspects of phenomenology and existentialism, and is now working on a study of intersubjectivity, and on a translation of the works of Emmanuel Levinas.

RAY HERBENICK is Assistant Professor at the University of Dayton and a graduate of Georgetown University. He is the author of articles on pragmatism, aspects of positivism, and Merleau-Ponty.

BERNARD FLYNN, a graduate of Duquesne University, is on the faculty of Empire College in New York. He is currently working on a study of Marxism.

JOSEPH BIEN, Assistant Professor at the University of Texas (Austin) studied at the University of Paris (Sorbonne), and is the translator of Merleau-Ponty's *Adventures of the Dialectic*. He is the editor of a series in political philosophy for the University of Texas Press.

DICK HOWARD is Assistant Professor at the State University of New York at Stony Brook and associate editor of *Telos*. He is the author of *The Development of the Marxian Dialectic*, editor of *Selected Writings of Rosa Luxemburg* and, with Karl Klare, of *The Unknown Dimension: Post-Leninist Marxism*. He has also written numerous articles on political thought.

RONALD BRUZINA, Assistant Professor at the University of Kentucky, is a graduate of Notre Dame University and a candidate at the University of Paris (Sorbonne). He is the author of *Logos and Eidos: The Concept in Phenomenology*.

1

Garth Gillan

IN THE FOLDS OF THE FLESH
PHILOSOPHY AND LANGUAGE

WHAT is the meaning of philosophy for Merleau-Ponty? And how does the discovery of that sense lead to the stance of philosophy within the world? In the thought of Merleau-Ponty, which spans the junctures of painting and psychology, language and history, politics and perception, ontology and linguistics, literature and anthropology, there is launched, through the destruction of positive philosophy and of phenomenology as the positive science of consciousness and its world, the idea of philosophy as the indirect and allusive language of the world. The initial importance of the idea of phenomenology for Merleau-Ponty lay in the way in which phenomenology provided an access to that domain of Being which philosophy perpetually interrogates and which it inhabits as the place of its own self-interrogation. For *The Visible and Invisible* philosophy is interrogation because Being exists in an interrogative manner. The question is a distinct way of knowing and not merely a preparation for a positive statement about the nature of things.

Consequently, in the thought of Merleau-Ponty, the idea of a return to the source of expression and thought entails a radicalization of the whole question of method and of the domain of experience to which the phenomenological method introduces thought. Thought is once again put to the test of a struggle with the meaning of being across the divergences, differences, and transitions which mark the perceptual and linguistic experience of the

1

world. That struggle for Merleau-Ponty has two foci: the language of philosophy and its self-discovery within the corporeal texture of language itself, the flesh of language. To be introduced to the thought of Merleau-Ponty means, at least, to follow the elliptical course of his thought as it moves, in the course of his development, around those two foci. It is that course that this introductory chapter will take.

The elaboration of the meaning of behavior for perceptual consciousness in *The Structure of Behavior* poses the question of philosophy within a return to the world of perception. The themes that form the inner essence of philosophy—existence, meaning, morality, and the significance of life and death—only take on the starkness and full impact of their reality in that experience where they erupt into consciousness in the most fundamental manner: the experience of perceptual consciousness. Only perceptual experience is the original and founding realm where existence, meaning, life, and death are concretely and directly met.[1] And it is from the structure of perceptual meaning that the questions about life and death take on their style and are directed toward the way in which philosophy must struggle with their density and impenetrability. Philosophical reflection finds its roots in coming face to face with phenomena, the appearances of meaning within perception, as the primary inscription of meaning into the unfinished text of the world.

Behavior reveals its meaning as structure because perceptual experience does not capture meaning through autonomous, sensible qualities or punctual atoms of sensory content. Perception or perceptual behavior reveals, rather, the physiognomy of the sensible. The sensible is meaningful not as a synthesis of originally disparate elements, but directly through its original appearance as an ensemble of relations, an original expressiveness that speaks out of the forms of perceptual objects as the human face speaks directly of the emotions and thoughts which animate it. To be meaningful, therefore, is to possess the coherency of a whole which expresses an autonomous configuration incapable of being reduced to its parts. It is a totality that emerges into significance before its parts as the physiognomy of the face emerges from the indistinct details of color and line.[2]

In the perceptual physiognomy of things, perception not only confronts meaning, but also, in the immediacy of that meaning and in its transcendence, the density and solidity of things.[3] The intimacy of things with perception, which is grounded in the way perception seizes their physiognomies, and the density and solidity which those same physiognomies express is what the word *phenomenon* translates. It expresses at once the ideality and the objectivity of perceptual meaning. But that intimacy and density do not only bind perception and sensibility; reflection, too, is bound by phenomena to become a phenomenology, "an inventory of consciousness as milieu of the universe."[4]

To be bound by a world that expresses itself within consciousness and to be a consciousness which is the expression of that world is to be an intentionality. The act of reflection is an intending of the perceived world. But, at the same time, it is not the perceived world; there is for it a domain of meaning other than itself. That domain arises through perception. Thus the relationship of reflection to what it reflects upon by bringing it to expression in language can only, for Merleau-Ponty, be interpreted within the relation of sign to signified. The sign and what it signifies, the signified, are tied together through an internal bond established in the act of expression. That bond, however, is not the relation of two separate elements in a one-to-one relationship. The sign expresses the signified; it is tied to the signified in the way that musical notation is the equivalent, on a different level, of the heard melody, and in the way that gestures translate musical notation into instrumental sounds; that is, not directly, but through the equivalences and lateral relations that constitute each set of signs. The sounds, inscriptions, and gestures do not signify each other in an absolute or direct manner, but only in terms of their relations to other gestures, sounds, and inscriptions. The internal bond between sign and signified is thus created within a system of equivalences brought about by relating differences, within a structure that merits the word *symbolic*.[5]

All of this means that, for *The Structure of Behavior*, philosophical reflection must be understood within that behavior that is characteristic of man: symbolic behavior. At that level, reflection is linguistic expression, language. Reflection discovers its reality in the act of expression which, rather than being a reflection of pregiven data, is the bringing forth of meaning, an act that brings into being a world of ideas. For *The Structure of Behavior* that act is the living word which constitutes the unity of word and concept. It is the meaning-bestowing word that actualizes the expression of meaning and in that manner unites language and reflection in the face of a common task: the expression of the world of sensibility. Therefore, to be authentic thought, thought living in the actuality of expression, reflection must be a phenomenology, the constituting *logos* of phenomena.[6]

It is at this juncture that phenomenology is an ontology, the question of the meaning of existence, for perception constitutes and grounds the world of intelligibility.[7] It is from the perceived world that the expressions of language gain their sense of being; language gains its right to speak of existence from perception, for it is perception that first teaches us what existence is. Perception is the original, unmediated relationship with existence, for it is within perception that what exists and is meaningful first appears. Existence is thus the category of the seen, the heard, the touched, the smelled, and the tasted. The role of perception as the realm of existence is identical to its role as the original domain of meaning. To be perceived is, for *The Structure of Behavior,* to exist, not in the sense that every vanishing shape possesses the density of things, but that the dense physiognomic character of things is the experience of their existence. Within perceptual consciousness, meaning translates existence as existence translates meaning, for to be meaningful is to carry the sense of being.[8]

Perception in *The Structure of Behavior* is a "naturizing thought"[9] which discloses a realm of meaning and existence to which language in its essence is committed. But it is also that which underscores the appearance of others as well as the appearance of things. In the order of symbolic behavior, perception and existence first belong to the appearances of others, but in such a way that the natural world of things and the intersubjective world of others are not ultimately two worlds. The experience of the thing and the intersubjective experience of others are both rooted in perception and thus are experiences or phenomena that take shape within the field of primordial nature.[10] From this perspective, the problem of perception for *The Structure of Behavior* is the presence in the perceptual world of meanings shared with others.[11] And, at the same time, it is only in terms of the intrinsic demands of the structure of perception, particularly the perspectival nature of the perception of things, that the weight of the question of the experience of others can be felt.

For *The Structure of Behavior,* then, the meaning of philosophy arises from the experience of truth, the truth of things and the truth of intersubjectivity—perception. Language as the medium within which reflection moves as its natural habitat commits philosophy to be a discourse about things: a phenomenology. In that sense *The Structure of Behavior* is a response to the demands of perceptual meaning and a turning of language toward phenomena which situates philosophical reflection, but without being, at the same time, an historical treatment of the question. The nature of the question about the meaning of philosophy stems, consequently, from a soil different from the soil of history. It is the onus of meaning that philosophy must bear and hence its structure must reflect the discourse to which it is committed by language: the discourse of things.

The preface to the *Phenomenology of Perception* is a more explicit discussion of the nature of philosophy, yet it, too, reflects the problematic of phenomenology which *The Structure of Behavior* discovered in the commitment of reflection to phenomena. While it is, on the one hand, a meditation on the questions around which Husserlian phenomenology gravitated—eidos, transcendental philosophy, the phenomenological reduction and the idea of a rigorous science—it is, on the other hand, an elaboration, again through the nature of language, of the phenomenological nature of philosophy in terms of a movement toward and from perceptual meaning. In the preface to the *Phenomenology of Perception* Merleau-Ponty confronts the question of the meaning of phenomenology in terms of the paradoxical manner in which the phenomenological experience poses the question of the meaning of subjectivity and the meaning of the world. In its moment of description, phenomenology is a return to the world as the source of meaning "of which knowledge always *speaks.*" [12] And the discovery of that world is also the discovery of perception as the consciousness in which subjectivity is dedicated to the world. That movement toward the pregiven world defines for Merleau-Ponty the sense of the phenomenological reduction, which, in opening up the question of the other, reveals the nature of thought as situated thought. Through the question of the other and through the world as the perpetual horizon of all *cogitationes,* the meaning of transcendental subjectivity lies within the experience of being structured by space and time. The movement from the meaning of the being of subjectivity and from the transcendental level is a movement to the meaning of the world and to the meaning of a subjectivity given to itself within the horizon of the world.

In addition phenomenology is a question of essences. It is not, however, a question of essences as separate objects of philosophy, but of essences as means by which access is gained to the things they signify. Essences are not separated from facts; there is not a world of essences and a world of facts; but facts demand an horizon of ideality in order to emerge into their significance. Language mediates that difference and, at the same time, insures that essences rest firmly upon the prepredicative life of consciousness. The essence is the significance of the fact. And in that manner it is also a return to the world in order to bring to light its facticity. In that facticity of the world, the eidetic reduction reaches the being of the world, its worldliness, its worldhood.

Through the concept of intentionality, which is not simply a reference to a possible object, but an operative intentionality in which consciousness is not act, but life, phenomenology is a phenomenology of origins which brings us into contact with the total intention or the style of being of a pebble or of a revolution. The concept of operative intentionality brings us to the level where thought originally comes into contact with the meaning of existence within history and which enables us to see the segments of history as "manifestations of a single existence." [13]

In opening up these avenues to the discovery of the being of the world, phenomenology for Merleau-Ponty incorporates a new notion of rationality. That concept of rationality in an inverse manner illuminates the significance of the preceding characterization of phenomenology. For it is in the fusion of perspectives, in the coming together of intersecting lines—the paths of my experiences and the paths of others' experiences—that the world appears. The meaning of the world is to be found in that fusion of perspectives as well as the emergence of reason—the coming to be of significance in the event. Philosophy is, therefore, installed within the world, not as an expression of something pregiven, but as a creative act that gives being. In its actuality it is part of the facticity of the world. Thus its task is to understand itself within the world and the world within it. The only preexistent *logos* is the world itself, which means that, as *logos*, as reason or rationality, the world encompasses the reference of the rationality expressed in philosophy, envelopes it, includes it within itself, so that the meaning of philosophy is also within the sense of the world, the horizon formed from the intersection of divergent paths.[14] To capture the world in its facticity is to seize it in its actuality, in its actual rationality, where meaning emerges in the event which, in turn, results from the convergence of the multitude of perspectives which compose and form the structure of the perceptual event.

What we want to retain from the preceding account is the structure of the approach to the question of the meaning of phenomenology and the characterization of the significance of the world and rationality. Phenomenology gains meaning for the *Phenomenology of Perception* in being centered within the juncture of world, self, and others.[15] Transcendental subjectivity is an intersubjectivity. The world is the emergence of meaning across things and across our encounters with other men. Its significance arises in its actuality and facticity as an event taking shape within those confrontations between subjectivity and things, between self and others. As a return to that world, phenomenology must situate itself in order to understand that world. No more eternal than the world, phenomenology is of the order of the event: it is a creative act that comes to take its place within the world, not as a preordained possibility, but as a part of the world as the existence of a different realm of expression within the world.

What makes that description of philosophy difficult is the idea of rationality which underlies the being of the world and the being of reason. Meaning is not positivity. There is no pregiven reason.

Why? Because meaning is the event, the moment of the fusion and convergence of perspectives in the appearance of the thing and the moment of the confrontation of countenances. Rationality arises and one can say there is meaning precisely at the moment of convergence and confrontation. Truth is nowhere else. Consequently meaning cannot be defined as a positive characteristic of things. Rather it is the experience of the convergence of divergent perspectives and situations.

Of major importance, also, is the fact that the movement of phenomenological reflection is viewed within the mediation which language effects between the horizon of ideality and the horizon of the world of perception. Language roots the significations which arise from the search for essences into the facticity of the world. Language is, in addition, the locus for the meditation upon the meaning of philosophy, as philosophy brings forth its own order or level of significance. At one stroke, therefore, language provides the focus for the interpretation to be given to the world of ideality and the means by which to ground that world within the one world it shares with perception.

The Structure of Behavior and the *Phenomenology of Perception* focus, as the document Merleau-Ponty submitted for his candidacy for a chair at the College de France tells us,[16] on the recovery of the world of perception whose emergence in behavior *The Structure of Behavior* established and whose meaning was explored in the *Phenomenology of Perception*. What they signified for the thought of Merleau-Ponty was an "archeology," the discovery of the structure of the perceived world. In that document one finds the things of the perceptual world described as "inexhaustible systems recognized in their style" and the world described as "the universal style shared in by all perceptual things" and as "an unfinished task." In addition the nature of subjectivity is considered in terms of the natal pact between the body and the world. In those passages are summarized the results of the "archeology" of perception.[17]

But, as the preface to the *Phenomenology of Perception* pointed out, counter to the horizon of the perceptual world is the horizon of ideality. And in that respect *The Structure of Behavior* and the *Phenomenology of Perception* are only the first steps in the elaboration of the tasks of philosophy. What remains to be done is to elaborate a theory of truth and a theory of intersubjectivity, areas which are present in *The Structure of Behavior* and the *Phenomenology of Perception,* but only in a tentative, fragmentary way. Subsequent works, the document tells us, are devoted to sketching out those areas in reaching beyond perception.

Those projected works will take up the questions of truth and of reflection in the same terms those questions were posed in the preface to the *Phenomenology of Perception*: through language. The verticality or depth of the spatial world, manifested in the act of designation or pointing, shows subjectivity to be a situation in contact with other situations. My situation opens out upon other situations through the gestures of the body. The theory of the mind shows the same structure—and hence the same actuality of universal thought—in being approached through language as expressive gesture. Language is a *diacritical* thought; its movement is lateral, in terms of the differences of words and the sense that appears within their junctures. It is through language that philosophy can move to a universal thought: the intersection of situated thoughts and their appeal to one another.[18]

Language also provides access to an understanding of symbolic systems or institutions as systems of exchange of thoughts or values, and to history as an intersubjective experience. What makes these systems possible is the mutual recognition of man by man—the recognition of a "fellow." The thought that emerges from that recognition is a transcendental man, the understanding of whom involves the *logos* of language and the *logos* of perception.[19] The existence of metaphysics is to be found in the juncture of those two *logoi,* not as the confrontation of two principles, Reason and Nature, but as the wonder involved in that act of expression which gathers together into a unity man, time, culture, and nature. The concept of expression is in that way the central category involved in the question of the essence of philosophy, for it joins language to perception and perception to language inasmuch as both together deliver the sense of the world and the sense of being.

The method of phenomenology, the document clearly states, is to be applied, in creating the problematic of truth and intersubjectivity, to the relation of man to man in language, knowledge, society, and religion. Thus there is a methodological continuity between the works taken up with the recovery of the world of perception as the origin of meaning and rationality and those works of the later period given over to the discovery of the way in which that truth comes to expression. But what is also clear is the central role which language has to play in defining the access to truth in those dimensions of being beyond the world of perception and which capitalizes on what the preface to the *Phenomenology of Perception* disclosed as the role of language as mediator between the world of ideality and the world of perception. Language is the situation of thought before the world and before other men.

The text we have been considering provides only a sketch of the direction in which the thought of Merleau-Ponty was moving prior to his assuming a chair at the Collège de France. And, at the same time, it only establishes certain heuristic concepts, for language, expression, transcendental man are not fully fleshed out expressions which contain in themselves the duration of philosophical discourse necessary to sustain their promise; they only signify the promise they contain. The question still remains as to what is the situation of thought. The constellation of questions opened up by that fundamental question is the subject of *In Praise of Philosophy*,[20] Merleau-Ponty's inaugural address at the Collège de France.

In Praise of Philosophy moves around two centers: the incarnation of meaning within the present—the present as the juncture of event and meaning—and the sense of expression. Lavelle prompts the discussion of the first and Bergson the discussion of the second. But the meaning of philosophy is to be found within both: its rationality is to be found within time and within the act of expression.

In the doctrine of intuition as coincidence with the duration of things and in that manner an intuitive grasp of absolute being, the philosophy of Bergson would seem to be a positivism, a subjection of thought and expression to what is and to what is without any distance between thought and being. What is in question in the interpretation of Bergson and Bergsonism is, for Merleau-Ponty, the progressive acquisition of that distance from things—a space for thought—within which being, perception, and thought can be considered in their interrelationships. For *In Praise of Philosophy*, perception originally creates that space. In perception is to be found the solicitation of being, its participation in us and our participation in it, so that our rapport with being is an oblique, lateral rapport with being, a rapport grounded by perception and one which opens us up to all the levels of being. There is within perception a "natural myth," our accord with all the dimensions of being. But that accord is matched by the fact that perception seems to come from the thing and emerges as the promotion of the thing to an existence for itself.[21]

An analogous relationship is to be found between consciousness and things at the level of philosophical discourse. The source of philosophical discourse demands that it be spoken and the philosopher speaks in order to bring it to expression. Hence philosophy is not coincidence, nor fusion with Being, but takes place within the space created by perception. If philosophy can be said to be an intuition, it thereby embodies a double reference: "first to the meaning it disengages from being and secondly to the silent being it interrogates."[22] Philosophy is generated where that meaning and that silent Being interpenetrate and communicate: the space of their accord. The space in which philosophy arises is that of a communication with meaning and with Being; or, as Merleau-Ponty says with emphasis, a reading, the art of seizing a meaning through a style before that meaning has been formulated into concepts and which, in addition, keeps in view the thing as the point where that meaning arises.

That reading, that act of expression, is in the eyes of Merleau-Ponty an original act which affirms its dependence on what antedates it, for in fact it antedates itself since it postulates as its condition for existence that it not only moves toward Being, but that Being moves toward it. And thus its full significance is to be found in the fact that it is an exchange in which meaning passes from one of the terms of that relation to the other, from expression to being and from Being to expression. Expression, philosophical expression, is a communication with Being, if one understands that word in its literal meaning, as a mutual passage, as a transference of sense within the space created by the difference which that transition presupposes.

A philosophy of expression never forgets that difference, for it can never forget that its abode is always situated within the act of expression, within the accord of the disengaged meaning and the thing and of the silent groping of the sense of the thing toward words. In positioning itself within that exchange, philosophy finds its original situation, for at the same time it is thrown into the embrace of intersubjectivity. Expression presupposes the one who speaks, the truth expressed, and the others to whom expression is directed. Philosophy and the nature of expression must satisfy all three conditions at once. And no point of that triangular set of relations can be eliminated without the act of expression and philosophy destroying their hold upon the world. The truth is not an idol, nor are others gods.[23]

There is for Merleau-Ponty in *In Praise of Philosophy* a risk and an enigma involved in the nature of philosophy, because philosophy tries to seize the sense of the world as it is interposed between the three points of that triangular relationship and to capture the significance of the event of meaning which forms at the point where the demands of the speaker, the demands of the truth, and the demands of others intersect. The risk is that the philosopher will end up being nowhere. Yet the task of philosophy requires and its principle of intelligibility demands that it remain suspended between truth, self, and others without deserting any of the ties that hold it fast. Being pulled in three directions at once gives to philosophy what Merleau-Ponty calls its malaise: [24] it seems to refuse to commit itself because it is committed to the sense of the world within its purview and it cannot go beyond that meaning without betraying itself.

Socrates is a major figure in *In Praise of Philosophy* as the symbolic expression of the situation of philosophical thought. Philosophy cannot escape its relationship to others; its adherence to them is one with its very existence. Thus the attitude it takes upon itself within the tensions of that adherence is one of irony: Socrates is philosophy "in his living rapport with the Athenians, in his absent presence, in his obedience without respect." [25] The philosopher in the person of Socrates does not change the world but sows the seeds of doubt among men and makes them uneasy about themselves and about their assurance which leads them to believe they have a firm hold on the truth. The presence of philosophy in the world is, from that perspective, an ironical presence, the presence of an absence and the absence of a presence. Nevertheless, for Merleau-Ponty it is the very ambiguity of this relationship between philosophy and the world that opens up within discourse an overture to the truth. It is the very awareness of the impossibility of absolute knowledge, a lacuna dwelling in the midst of consciousness, that drives philosophy toward truth. Yet the essence of the philosophical endeavor does not consist of that consciousness by itself.

To allow the lack of absolute knowledge to seep into the soul of the philosopher and corrode his relationship to the truth would be to make of skepticism the inner limits beyond which thought could not pass. As a search philosophy implies, for Merleau-Ponty, that "there are things to see and to say." [26] Where is philosophy to find those things to be seen and to be said? That question brings us back to the first theme encountered in *In Praise of Philosophy*: the incarnation of meaning in the contingency of the event. To come face to face with meaning structured by the radical historicity or temporalization of the event is to witness the birth of meaning in the life of perception and in the act of expression. The center of philosophical interrogation for Merleau-Ponty is not located in the question of a source of meaning residing outside of time or beyond the confines of the finite world, nor in a destiny given by a theological interpretation of human existence. Philosophy is neither theology nor antitheology; it is of an entirely different order, because the source it interrogates lies elsewhere—within the dimensions, perceptual and expressive, of the world.[27]

But if God is not a positive concept for philosophy in the eyes of Merleau-Ponty, neither is the concept of humanity in the sense of a datum given beforehand which could subsequently be utilized as a principle of explanation. Man or humanity is not an independent force which serves as its own justification; rather, man is the place where the lines of meaning forming the texture and patterns of the world intersect.[28] In man, rationality—the emergence of meaning and hence truth within the divergence of perspectives—has a natal *topos*, a place of birth; man is the abode of the nativity of truth. History, too, is not a positive concept, a pregiven datum whose interpretation would provide an unassailable foundation for the construction of philosophy, for it, too, in its intelligibility is governed by the contingency of the event. For Merleau-Ponty, thought does not start with universal history, since rather than signifying the inception of historical reason, the idea of universal history is a slackening of the ties between thought and the contingency of history. The universality of truth is not a given, but, on the contrary, emerges from the intersection of men's lives and from the appeal of one human life to another.

In its perspectival finitude and irreducible contingency, the event is the genesis and source of reason. That means that, as meaning assumes concrete forms in history and in the world of coexistence, it is riddled through with negativity—with the nonpositive structure of the contingent, temporal event. And philosophy, in recognizing its source in the rationality whose emergence springs from that event, assumes in the structure of its own expressive nature that negativity. The significations that philosophy seeks and the significations that it finds are not preinscribed into a world completely realized and bearing within itself its own consummation before the advent of the spoken word. The spoken word completes the passage of the world to the expression of its meaning and truth and therefore, in a countermovement, the spoken word is inscribed into the structure of the world. For Merleau-Ponty what must be understood in coming to comprehend the sense of philosophy is that the meaning of philosophy arises from a situation: the juncture of philosophy and the perceptual birth of meaning in the midst of a world never completed and always remaining an unfinished task. The problems and difficulties attendant upon every attempt to understand that situation proceed from the fact that only within the world does the act of expression have Being, and yet in a retroactive manner it contributes to the meaning of Being at the very moment that it brings it to expression.

To understand philosophy for Merleau-Ponty is first of all, consequently, to understand that it takes its intelligibility from the act of expression *in rapport* with the perceptual birth of meaning, and that it installs itself within that juncture and not on only one side of it. And, secondly, to understand philosophy is to see that the source of meaning, what is spoken and seen within that juncture, is not a positive signification, but a lateral sense. Meaning erupts in the convergence of divergent perspectives within the perceptual event and, in addition, "universal" meaning erupts in the exchange of meaning and values in language, history, and culture. Meaning is divergence, separation, and difference. And philosophy's hold upon the truth is within that act of expression which preserves in its own diacritical structure and at another level the divergence, separation, and difference which characterize meaning within perception.

The fact that philosophy installs itself within language—finds there its course of intelligibility—is also reflected in Merleau-Ponty's attitude toward the world of action and to politics. For Merleau-Ponty at the time of *In Praise of Philosophy,* philosophy strictly speaking has no task in the world proper to it alone. No absolute mission has been communicated to philosophical thought by divine intent, nor by a reading of history pointing to the irreversible progress of mankind. It is the absence of such a positive source and origin that gives to philosophy a certain tragic aura. Not enrooted in a dimension of being other than its own rapport with the life of perception, the philosophical endeavor cannot absolve itself of the tensions and contradictions which arise within it; rather, it must bear those contradictions itself by assuming them as the very conditions of its existence.[29]

For the philosopher to speak is an act. Yet there remains a radical difference between that act of expression and action itself. To speak of action is not the same as engaging oneself through action in the byways and detours of the political milieu. And for philosophy that difference is telling for it prevents the philosopher from being a "real being" for Merleau-Ponty, since he must by the very meaning of his situation take a distance from the man of power. Nevertheless, the necessity of assuming that distance does not reverse the relationship of the philosopher to human existence; rather, the distance separating language and action is a sign of human existence. That distance is carved into the situation of every man as the difference between the need to understand and the need to choose, between comprehension and decision. Far from being a conflict created by two separate faculties vying for domination over the being of man, that difference consists in a tension to be found in the twistings and turnings by which men come to terms with their own existence and struggle with the fact that reality outstrips understanding, and at the same time in understanding real situations men see beyond the confines of their limited historical present. That difference and distance from the world of action signifies another dimension of philosophical expression: irony. For the philosopher irony is not an alibi but a modality of expression, the way that philosophy takes up its presence in the world. Symbolized by Socrates, irony does not signify that the philosopher is elsewhere, but, on the contrary, that he is somewhere, that he consciously lives within the limitations of expression and within the finite conditions of the truth such as he has experienced it. What that attitude signifies is the expressive presence among men proper to philosophy—to speak and, in speaking, to be among men.[30]

Although written some six years later, what Merleau-Ponty said of the philosophical attitude of irony in *In Praise of Philosophy* recapitulates what he wrote in 1946 at the time of his active political involvement with *Les Temps Modernes*. Reflecting upon the relations between Marxism and philosophy, Merleau-Ponty wrote:

But if the philosopher knows this, if he assigns himself the task of pursuing the immanent logic of other experiences and other existences instead of putting himself in their place, if he forsakes the illusion of contemplating the totality of completed history and feels caught up in it like all other men and confronted by a future *to be made,* then philosophy fulfills itself by doing away with itself as isolated philosophy. This concrete thinking, which Marx calls "critique" to distinguish it from speculative philosophy, is what others propound under the name "existential philosophy." [31]

Confronted with the urgency of the demand and need for political action, the sense of philosophy both in 1953 and 1946 requires on the part of the philosopher an attitude of hesitation and one of taking one's time, since to rush to conclusions would be to betray serious thought for the spectacular.[32] Philosophy cannot be other than what it is and to be itself it must reflect within the movements of its own discourse its true situation: the way that philosophy exists among men and shares their existence is through language.

To speak is a heavy burden; irony is a presence that weighs heavily upon language.

In *In Praise of Philosophy* all the themes that are summed up in the idea of irony as the positive presence which philosophy has to the world and which issues from its own negativity prefigure with concrete contours what *The Visible and the Invisible* terms the interrogative being of philosophy. In *The Visible and the Invisible* the interrogative style of philosophy—the manner of knowing which is structurally a question—traverses the many levels at which the problematic of that work moves; it is a progressive recapitulation and retrograde movement. For *The Visible and the Invisible* the question of philosophy stands between two other questions, the significance of the history of philosophy and the significance of Being. And the question itself finds its structure in being suspended between those two polar questions. It is itself a meditation upon the way it gains access to the level of experience at which reality takes on its primordial meaning.

It is clear that the text of *The Visible and the Invisible* moves along those axes, the history of philosophy and the interrogation of Being. The first of those axes cannot be looked upon as a mere matter of stylistic expediency, an artifice contrived to allow words to gain their momentum and to permit the argument to find its own center. Nor is it an introduction which would lead into the major question only to be cast off as an arbitrary preparation. The introductory reflections in *The Visible and the Invisible* on the history of philosophy—on historical forms of philosophical reflection—are, rather, the very centering of the fundamental question of philosophy, the naming of Being. To see the necessity of that introduction which rests upon the allusive and lateral structure of expression which implies its mediation through other texts and other ways of framing the question of Being, we must first examine the proto-thought of *The Visible and the Invisible,* the working notes to that text.

One of the first notes written in February 1959 recalls the manner in which the question of the meaning of philosophy was phrased in the preface to the *Phenomenology of Perception.* The all-encompassing sense of philosophy cannot be that of a "creation

(*Gebilde*) resting upon itself." Philosophy cannot be an autonomous creation, since it has for its end the expression of that which truly is "of itself"—for whom to be and to be autonomous are the same thing—the life-world (*Lebenswelt*). What is important to note in this manner of posing the question of the significance of philosophy is that the polarization created by the juxtaposition of a creative thought and an autonomous world is not the framework into which Merleau-Ponty thinks that the question can be properly put. The direction, rather, in which the meaning of philosophy must be sought is indicated by focusing the question upon the point where the two levels or dimensions of the question—the idea of creative philosophy and that of an autonomous world—intersect with and envelop each other: "What there is is a creation that is called forth and engendered by the *Lebenswelt* as operative, latent historicity, that prolongs it and bears witness to it—." [33]

The note on the "Origin of Truth" dated January 1959 reveals the import of speaking of the life-world (*Lebenswelt*) as latent historicity. The *logos* of the life-world (*Lebenswelt*) is situated across and beneath the constructions of scientific understanding. For beneath the historicity of truth as conceived by the scientific tradition created by Descartes—truth as an infinite task—there is an "organic history." Hence, what creative philosophy responds to at the level of language is a sense of the world lying beneath linear, horizontal history. The truth that philosophy encounters is not one that is laid out before it and that recedes into the ever-distant future as an elusive goal, but, on the contrary, one that continually "*sustains it from behind.*" [34] The historical dimensions of truth lie within that history operative in each act of expression, as the body as the ensemble of habitual operations underscores every personally initiated gesture, and as language as a system of signs underscores every individual act of expression.

As a succeeding note, dated February 1959, states, the first part of *The Visible and the Invisible* was projected as a reflection upon the historical meaning of philosophy, an historical *Selbstbesinnung*, which would uncover signs within that historical sense leading from nonphilosophy to philosophy itself. [35] That historical self-understanding on the part of philosophy operates, not at the level of objective history—the linear, accumulative history of philosophy —but within "organic history" or what the notes also term "vertical history" in which, in opposition to the mere succession of philosophical systems, there is "between philosophies a perceptual relation or a relation of transcendence." [36] That conception of vertical history lies opposed to the conception of linear, objective history, since within it philosophies communicate with each other and there is a basis upon which each can contest the expressions of the other. And that, moreover, is only possible because within vertical history they are sustained by the same expressive Being, by the life-world (*Lebenswelt*) as operative historicity. To a linear model for the conceptualization of the history of philosophy, Merleau-Ponty opposes a mode of understanding in which the relations between succeeding philosophies are not on the same plane; those relations exist at different depths and compose divergent meaning-strata. Yet within that stratification along the vertical axis of history, each mode of philosophical expression contains an intrinsic and self-sustaining reference to Being. That means that every philosophy must be understood as an interrogation of the field of existence which it shares with all the rest. Philosophy consists, then, in "circles that include one another." [37]

Merleau-Ponty characterizes this historical self-understanding of philosophy not as a view upon history, or a view upon the history of philosophy. It is an historical view, true, but one that eliminates the perspective of points of view; it is a *structural* elucidation of the sense of history, a history beyond the relativity of perspectives found in historicism. In this structural interpretation of history—a history beyond historicism—the history of philosophy is "not the event of such and such a philosophy as a *creation* and a *solution* of 'problems,' but this philosophy situated within the hieratic ensemble of Being and the existential eternity, i.e., within an *interrogative* ensemble which, like Lefort's *Machiavelli*, is not a dogmatism." [38] Hence, three elements form the matrix of this structural history: the hieratic ensemble of Being, existential eternity, and interrogative ensemble. Caught up in the threads of each other, none of these concepts is sufficient of itself to render the sense of vertical history, but together they decenter the view of history as linear progress.

What emerges is not the structure of progress, but the structure of communication, the transference and interpenetration of expressed and perceived meanings.

For Merleau-Ponty in the texts of *The Visible and the Invisible* the meaning of Being is not a positive concept capable of a definition encompassing definite boundaries, nor is it a positive experience that, as a figure emerging clearly from the ground of human experience, could render ontology actual. On the contrary, the sense of Being for Merleau-Ponty lies across the expressive and perceptual experience of the life-world (*Lebenswelt*) as a stratified and differentiated expanse. The meaning of that expanse lies within a history, within a process of differentiation which realizes itself as the coming to be of divergent strata of meaning, of contrasting regions of experience and opposing levels of visibility. It is the enrooting of existence within that hieratic act—the emergence and duration of divergent and contrasting levels and planes of meaning in language and in perception—and hence within a differentiated and expansive temporal *now* which gives and grounds the meaning of time and the sense of the present.

Being escapes; not only the point at which lines and expressions intersect in the perceptual world and in speech, Being is also the intimation in each thing seen and spoken of things yet to be seen and said. It is not only the figure and the ground whose unity comprises the perceptual field, but also the passage from one to the other, the interval between them, the movement from one to the other which is a permanent tension in the perceptual field and is what makes things visible. As an expanse of meaning, Being consequently is both the visible and the invisible, the strands of sense that run from being to being and render them visible and expressive. The stance of Being is that of a question: in their visibility and in their expressive character, things ask of the eye and hand what can be seen and touched, and of language what can be said. The interrogative mode of Being lies within its visibility and invisibility and in the difference between them that is bridged when a thing is seen or a word spoken. Therefore: *"One cannot make a direct ontology. My 'indirect' method (being in the beings) is alone conformed with being—'negative philosophy' like 'negative theology.'"* [39]

A strange conception of history is this vertical history of the world and of Being, and one that lies at a distance from the philosophy of history inasmuch as the idea of history lies too closely bound up with individual praxis and thus makes it tempting to take the dimension of the historicity of Being to be that of individual action.[40] It is not individual action that provides the grounding for the history of Being. What does provide that foundation for Merleau-Ponty lies beneath the association of persons across the moments of history and the divisions of geography in the original foundation of space in time and of time in space—a "carnal Urhistorie" as the nexus of history and transcendental geology revealed in the being of the flesh.[41]

The *Urstiftung,* the primordial foundation of Being in the flesh which that carnal, primitive history encompasses, is at once a taking up of Being and a laying down of Being in its strata, in the levels of meaning which in their divergence, difference, and differentiation constitute the Being of the world. That is what it means to locate the primordial history of Being at the nexus of history and transcendental geology, for history signifies the taking up of meaning, the act of transcendence, in opposition to the sedimentation of meaning—and hence the laying down of meaning in geological (carnal) strata—into the epochs of its antiquity. Caught in the movement of time, the interrogation of Being cannot forget that at the foundation of Being there is an original forgetting, an original passivity to be found in the existence of the past, at the same time that there is an original sense of the future. What thought has thus uncovered is an uncultivated terrain, not directly history or culture, but the tissue of history and culture which forms the matrix into which human actions and intentions are inscribed. First expressed in *The Structure of Behavior* as primordial nature, this terrain of philosophical thought is in *The Visible and the Invisible* termed the intertwining or chiasm, the very nature of Being: ". . . every relation with being is *simultaneously* a taking and a being taken, the hold is held, it is *inscribed* and inscribed in the same being that it takes hold of." [42]

As a relation to Being lived within the expressive nature of language, philosophy is itself, therefore, an experience of an inscription into Being. Its relationship to itself in the sense of the type of self-reflection it requires as a mode of discourse is realized on the same level as any and all relations to Being—it is not outside of the world, viewing the world as a transcendental spectator, but is itself a contribution to the sense of the world. And in that respect the dimensions of the question of philosophy in the working notes to *The Visible and the Invisible* continue the idea of philosophy announced in the preface to the *Phenomenology of Perception*. Philosophy is a laying down of Being and an assumption of meaning within language as an inscription into Being: language inscribes philosophical reflection into the tissue of the world and bestows upon it the stark reality usually associated with the transcendent and alien character of things. Within its own expressive nature philosophical reflection encounters the very terrain to which it had been called to expression by the interrogative stance of the perceptual and cultural world. The burden of philosophy is to describe and discover the supports of meaning which lie not on the surface but in the vertical depths of the world: "The essential is to describe the vertical or wild Being as that pre-spiritual milieu without which nothing is thinkable, not even the spirit, and by which we pass into one another, and ourselves into ourselves in order to have *our own* time. It is philosophy alone that gives it—" [43]

The course that we have followed through the subterranean passages of *The Visible and the Invisible* has revealed that the structure of the question concerning the meaning of philosophy is derived from the very terrain that philosophical discourse occupies. Its structure encompasses the two foci that every relation to being encompasses: history or transcendence and transcendental geology or the sedimentation of meaning. It is the continual passage between these two axes which constitutes for Merleau-Ponty the nature of philosophy as interrogation, a knowledge or nonknowledge, a type of knowledge which differs structually from the judgment that asserts or posits Being. For philosophy, the question does not merely anticipate a positive relationship to being expressed in the form of a judgment; rather, only the question involves the very manner in which philosophy is itself a relation to Being. The interrogative structure of Being solicits an indirect and allusive discourse that signifies across the silences of language instead of limiting itself to the narrow confines of positive meaning.

Yet is it possible that interrogation is merely a hesitant and circumspect judgment, a judgment, finally, in the interrogative mode? To answer that question in a positive manner would be to contradict the formal nature of the judgment as assertion. A judgment that hesitates, that is conscious of the finitude that surrounds its every move still has the form of an assertion; only it has become an assertion of probability or of possibility. From this perspective, a question is merely the anticipation of positive knowledge; or it raises for positive knowledge the specter of inadequacy and thus creates an original impulse that carries consciousness toward an explicit formulation of the way things are. From Descartes to Husserl the interrogative form of the question as methodic doubt or phenomenological reduction has provided the philosophical method by which the world becomes an object for investigation. But no more than an overture, it has not seeped into the very structure of knowledge: from doubt, philosophy, so armed against criticism, has turned to assertion.

If, for Merleau-Ponty, philosophy as interrogation radically separates itself from that tradition, it does so by taking the proper moment of philosophical discourse to be its beginning—the moment it engages in the struggle for expression in the face of the silent world of perception. Philosophy, as the preface to the *Phenomenology of Perception* discloses, is a return to the origin, to the commencement of expression before the facticity—the worldhood—of the world. The idea of interrogation deepens that description of philosophy in elaborating philosophical discourse as the manner of speaking for which that return constitutes a unique style. The question is that commencement, for the question not only captures for a brief moment the birth of meaning in the coeval foundation of consciousness in the world and the world in consciousness, but sustains it, prolongs it into a mode of knowing that lies beneath the modes of knowing dominated by the assertive form of the judgment. And as a return to the commencement of expression—what Merleau-Ponty also speaks of as original speech *(parole parlante)* —the interrogative mode of knowing is criticism, a hyperreflection which signifies in its expressions the relationship between philosophical discourse and the world which is there to be spoken. In that discourse, Being is constantly present as that which is perpetually addressed, heeded to, and never satisfied:

> But already when I say "what do I know?" in the course of a phrase, another sort of question arises: for it extends to the idea of knowing itself; it invokes some intelligible place where the facts, examples, ideas I lack, should be found; it intimates that the interrogative is not a mode derived by inversion or by reversal of the indicative and of the positive, is neither an affirmation nor a negation veiled or expected, but an original manner of aiming at something, as it were a *question-knowing*, which by principle no statement or "answer" can go beyond and which perhaps therefore is the proper mode of our relationship with Being, as though it were the mute or reticent interlocutor of our questions.[44]

The sense of philosophy, therefore, is not to be found in analyzing the world into indecomposable elements and reconstructing them according to a rational model, nor does it terminate in a mute acknowledgment of Being; rather it is to be found in the attempt to sustain, through the twists and turns of language, the relationship to Being and to the world that has called it forth from silence. Philosophy remains perpetually a question because it speaks its presence to the crystallization of meaning in the visible events of the gaze and in the audible events of the spoken word. It articulates the immanent logic of those events which manifest themselves as certain "general powers"—in a style of if . . . then—and which, in addition, reveal themselves as traces of the Passage of Being. Each event in perception and in language is not a world closed in upon itself, a unique individuality impermeable to the transference of sense from thing to thing and from word to word which characterizes it. Rather, each event gives evidence of that transference of sense and hence of a certain style that words and perceived things possess and which gives them their verbal or perceptual sense. In the aura of generality which surrounds things and words there is for Merleau-Ponty a testimony to the hold of Being over beings, a prepossession of meaning-events, that is expressed in those powers and styles which "continue to institute the new there." [45] Those general styles or structural laws are relations of prepossession, recapitulation, and overlapping which open individual beings onto a new kind of being, a "porous being" called by Husserl an horizon.[46]

"Question-knowing" hence is not a cognition, since its entry into the dispersed field of Being is not one which characterizes that of a question for which there would be a specific answer. To that interrogation there corresponds not an answer but "a confirmation of its astonishment." [47] Perception—or the faith of perception—is first of all that interrogative thought, for perception does not posit Being but haunts the movements and points of convergence that constantly remake themselves to make of each new landscape a new mapping of the perceptual world, but yet one that in its style and the power of the gaze over the things that populate it carries with it the sense of belonging to one world. Solicited by this dispersion and recollection of Being, by this interrogative way in which things exist in the perceptual world, "philosophy is the perceptual faith questioning itself about itself." [48] For it is that perceptual faith that in its hold upon wild Being first introduces us into the realm of truth and first tells us of our contact with Being—a certitude beyond justification.

The language of philosophy, consequently, is the promotion of that tenacious hold upon the truth of things perceived—perceptual faith—to the level of expression where that relationship to Being is a question for itself, where it is a perpetual self-interrogation. Far from dissipating that faith by turning it into knowledge and decomposing the savage Being of the world that it unfolds into a universe of rational entities, philosophy for Merleau-Ponty continues the interrogation of the world initiated in the first movements of the gaze and sustains within language the sense of Being permeating the stark confrontation with things begun by perception.[49] In language philosophy continues and sustains the very articulation and dispersion which constitutes the structure of the wild Being of perception; inscribed into Being it continues the ontogenesis of Being: ". . . philosophy is operative language, that language that can be known only from within, through its exercise, is open upon the things, called forth by the voices of silence, and continues an effort of articulation which is the Being of every being." [50]

The original act of philosophy is to interrogate the experience of

Being in the faith of perception and to question that experience with respect to its essence or, rather, since it is the original meaning of essences not to be intuitions, but to be experiences which feel within themselves the weight of the Being they think, to feel the full weight of that experience within the turns of its discourse.[51] Philosophy thus is the dimension of expression where a *what* appears: the *what* of the coming to be of Being within the mutual involvement and exchange of the body and things—the flesh—within the brute experience of the world and the *what* that issues into a language that experiences in the weight of its own words the reality of which it speaks. Not only the question of "who am I" or not even that, philosophy is, in the end, the question of *"what is there"* and "what is *the there is."* Philosophical discourse does more than indicate a being which it takes for its object; it opens up within the passage of its own language the dimensions of Being first disclosed in perception before the advent of the spoken word. Philosophy is a way of inhabiting the world by following the course of Being as it articulates itself within its dispersion among beings and between perception and language. It, too, in its submission to the expressive power of language is a trace of Being.

The conclusion forces itself upon us, then, that it is not only the specific demands of philosophical discourse which introduce us to the element of thought within which Merleau-Ponty locates the interrogation of Being. Language itself mediates that introduction, as it mediates in the preface to the *Phenomenology of Perception* the transition from ideality to facticity and from facticity to ideality which characterizes the structure of meaning in the lived world. It is in language that the strangeness of the world—the experience from which philosophy takes its origins—is turned into the struggle for expression. The fate of truth and rationality thus depends upon the traces of sense in the bond between the signifying and the signified. Language for Merleau-Ponty does not bear the sole responsibility for the origins of rationality, but it does bear the responsibility for historical rationality, that is, for the existence or nonexistence of the transcendence of historical contingency.

The structure of meaning within perception repeats itself, for Merleau-Ponty, within language. Meaning within language is diacritical; that is to say, the sense expressed by the spoken word exists between words, in their divergences from one another, and not in a unitary meaning bestowed upon the sound stratum of speech by acts of consciousness, as is the case for Husserl. Spread out along the passage of discourse, meaning thus is immanent to language; the word *has* its meaning as Merleau-Ponty affirms in the *Phenomenology of Perception* within the first few pages of the chapter devoted to "the body as expression and speech." This having meaning, this particular way that the spoken word possesses meaning, expresses the manner in which there is a subjectivity of language.[52] And hence it plunges language immediately into the realm of that anonymous and impersonal course of consciousness which bears the name of the habitual body. The spoken word is only one way in which the power of expression which resides in man is realized.[53] And it, too, is a manifestation—as is the symbolic body—of existence, a modulation of the fundamental manner in which the subject is present to the world and to his own life.[54]

Language, consequently, is in the world as the body is in the world. But more importantly, the way that the word has meaning refers to the manner in which meaning inhabits the perceiving subject as already open to the world with the first act of perception and as an adherence to a perceptual field. That overture of the perceiving body to the world and its specific being as an adherence to a perceptual field carry with them the sense of the past. The body has meaning, because as an operative and habitual presence to the world it already has meaning; in its actual movements, the body is sensitive to meanings which weigh it down as the perpetual sedimentation of the past. The body, or the perceiving subject, *has* meaning since it is the adherence to a field of sense that it has not created and which gives it a center other than itself. And so the spoken word has meaning, since what it expresses is other than itself: the world of perception.

More specifically, what is that mode of possession at the level of the body? How does meaning inhabit the body as the general and habitual intentionality of the world? That intentionality is an expressiveness, for the perceiving gestures which comprise the "motor intentionality" of the body have the body as corporeal schema as their horizon and background. They coalesce into a significance which is immanent to them and live that significance from within because the manner in which they inhabit their space—the hand, the eye—is the figuring of that meaning, its corporeal configuration. The acts of the body are expressive because they signify, not in a literal, self-contained manner, but because, in an indirect, mediated manner, through being a way of modulating existence, they are ways of living a rapport with an object instead of being isolated responses to absolute stimuli. The body as the corporeal schema, as a postural hold upon itself and upon its own space, is the field of equivalences in which gestures in their meaning are capable of substitution, one for the other. And it is that body which grounds the expressive character of its gestures, for it is the horizon and perceptual ground in which each gesture as a divergence from other gestures and in turn a relation to them is a corporeal configuration and hence a physiognomy.

In that way the body is an expressive space and, moreover, the very movement of expression.[55] It literally gives a place to perceptual meanings by locating them, through the perceiving movements of its separate organs, in its perceptual field and by making them exist like things—under our hands and under our eyes. The gestures of the body create an expressive space as the gestures of the auger create a space—a temple—by setting off definite boundaries and as certain movements effected by the hand of the painter translate themselves into a definite texture of the canvas—a brushstroke that in the character that it gives to the sense of colors and lines on the canvas is the sign of a painter's style, the manner in which he uses his hands. If that is true of aesthetic gestures, that is because in their motricity, the parts of the body are consecrated to action [56] and are so in the manner of an habituality, of an already accessible space which underscores and gives density to the fleeting actions of the present.

The subjectivity of the perceiving body is thus incapable of being comprehended in an analysis which would engender its principal momentum from an interpretation of consciousness as a totality of acts and as the activity of self-consciousness—the cogito. The failure of the interpretation of corporeal consciousness as self-consciousness is exactly the moment at which philosophy gains access to the type of presence to the world which defines the subjectivity of perception. Consciousness is not first of all consciousness and in being consciousness a relation to itself—in Kant's terms, the transcendental unity of apperception—and only subsequently open to the world. Rather it is open from the very beginning, for it is as an overture to the world, as the horizon of things, that corporeal consciousness gains its essential structure and essence. With respect to the nature of carnal consciousness, then, the structure of self-consciousness is a later acquisition and in determining the being of consciousness merely an afterthought.

These reflections make clear to some extent the place of the major exposition of the nature of perception in the *Phenomenology of Perception*. Strangely enough the major exposition of the nature of perception is not to be found, Merleau-Ponty informs us, in the pages devoted to the spatiality and motility of the body which provide the main themes for the discussion of the body as the movement of expression. On the contrary, the major interpretation of the nature of perception lies beyond the thematic considerations given to the body and is situated in the second part of the *Phenomenology of Perception*—in the problematic of the perceived world. It is at the level of the kind of meaning or sense realized within the gestural movements of perception—the type of meaning inhabiting perception—and in the themes concentrated on that level of discussion that the phenomenology of perception possesses complete significance. The phenomenology of perception, for Merleau-Ponty, is an analysis of the sense realized in perceptual acts and not principally an analysis concentrating upon the characteristics belonging to perception as an act, cogito, or apperception. Within the limits of the cogito, consciousness does have a specific function to fulfill as an act, since in being distinct from the object and untouched by it, it is the process in which both the unity of its object and its own unity are assured. On the other hand, the perceiving body has no specific function in the sense just referred to, since it is inhabited with meaning, modified by it and, most importantly, because it is not an act. Its unity is assured not by its own synthesis but by the unity of time, by a general spontaneity which is the very course run by consciousness without being the product of its active syntheses. Subject and object, as Merleau-Ponty states in the chapter on temporality, are two abstract moments of a "unique structure which is presence."

The body and the world form a system of equivalences and do not stand in a frontal confrontation, each in opposition to the other. As the articulation of the perceptual field—and the perceptual world—follows with the gestural movements of the body, so the movements of the body are articulations of the perceptual field; in the differentiations of that field is to be found their sense. Things solicit, through the interplay of light and shadows, the contrast of planes, and the perpetual contrast of figure and ground, the actions of the body and, in turn, their sensible texture is the term of the gestures which explore them. "The thing, and the world, are given," Merleau-Ponty writes, "to me along with the parts of my body, not by any 'natural geometry,' but in a living connection comparable, or rather identical with that existing between the parts of my body itself." [57] Things vary in terms of the movements of the body and the perceptions of the body vary in terms of things, "because they are the two facets of one and the same act." [58] The regions of the body intercommunicate, sight with touch, and touch with sight; they transfer their meanings from one to the other, just as the texture of the perceived thing bestows a particular hue upon the color it possesses. The perceptions of the body can be and are translated into the perceptions of things, as the perceptions of things can be and are translated into the perceptions of the body.

The sensible, therefore, takes possession of the body as a mode of behavior by soliciting the complicity of the body in its motricity as the body begins to initiate a motor response to the sensible issuing into perception. With the eyes focused at a distance, the two images of the finger held up before the eyes both feel the prick of a needle, or the prick of the needle is felt in two places. Colors have a certain motor presignification in some diseases of the cerebellum or frontal cortex, so that red and yellow lead to movements toward the center of the body and blue and green to movements away from the body toward the external world. At the level of motricity, then, the sensible invades the body by involving its actions and support even before the perception in question has clarified itself and in the form of an initial movement of the body toward perception: ". . . the sensible has not only a motor and vital significance, but is nothing other than a certain way of being in the world suggested to us from some point in space and seized and acted upon by our body, provided that it is capable of doing so, so that sensation is literally a form of communion." [59] To commune with the world—to bestow upon the world a sacramental value—to coexist with the world—those three expressions are the forms of expression in which Merleau-Ponty tries to express what was originally discovered in the solicitation of motor activity by the elements figuring in the structure of the sensible. More than metaphors, they point to the meaning that perception and the perceived have beyond and beneath the alternatives of the for-itself and the in-itself.

The solicitation of perception by the texture of the perceived, the taking possession of the body by the sensible through the very motricity of the body, signifies that the perceived is more than a sensible quale; it is a type of behavior. Only subsequently and through acts of attention can the sensible be split up into local areas of meaning—color, shape, surface, etc.—with definite limits. To perceive is to take up a posture before the object. And in that posture the body in its actions is bound by the object, as the object in its sensible dimensions is bound to the body. That interchange and exchange means that "the sensible gives to me what I have loaned to it, but it is from it that I have taken it." [60] Perception is thus not the bestowing of meaning upon the perceived thing, but a dialogue between the body and the thing from which issues the sensible meaning crystallizing between the reciprocal horizons of the body and the world.

Just as the body is an expressive space and the gestures of the body possess expressive meaning as configurations upon its postural presence to itself, the sensible meaning that is perceived within the thing and within perception is indistinguishable from the perceiving movements in which it comes to be, for as sensible meaning it too is an expressive unity. It is a physiognomy and an organism. It is so, first of all, in the sense that it arises as the resolution of tensions in the perceptual field—within the structure of figure-ground but also in such a manner that makes it possible to say that the sky "thinks itself in me," [61] and that perception raises the perceived to the level of an existence for itself. The sensible is not a positive given, but appears in the form of a gestalt, an expressive unity arising through the interaction of its parts and not through sensible qualia given once and for all and without internal modulation. It is that internal modulation which corresponds within the sensible thing to the system of equivalences existing between the gestures of the body and, therefore, accounts for the unity of the perceived and perception in sharing the sense of the sensible. The tension existing between the different parts of the sensible thing—the gestalt—is literally the "sensibility" of each part to the others and a quasi knowledge on the part of each of the dynamics of the whole. [62]

The sensible, therefore, has a mode of being that, far from separating it from perception, joins it to perception. Both share a common manner of articulating their being principally due to the fact that they have the same origin in the presence of sensible meaning. Perception and the sensible escape the dichotomy of the for-itself and the in-itself inasmuch as the presence of which they are abstract moments is elaborated at the level of the impersonality and habituality of the body's prereflective hold upon the world. To begin with, "every perception takes place in an atmosphere of generality and is given to us as anonymous." [63] It is not the personal, voluntary *I* that initiates and carries out the operations of the perceiving body. Those operations lie beneath volition and the responsibility characteristic of personal acts. It is true to say, as Merleau-Ponty does, that in perception "one" perceives. In that respect, the subject of perception is of the same nature as the subject of birth and death, for each perception is a birth and a death inasmuch as it is unique and one of its kind. Secondly, perception is anonymous, because it is never complete or at an end. There is a world beyond the world which I touch and look upon at the present moment. The world, then, is transcendent; it is always beyond what I actually see, hear, and touch or, more precisely, what I see, hear, and touch have a transcendence—a being always beyond—that constantly eludes me and places me on this side of their complete sense. In addition, the hand and the eye are organs which, in circumscribing specialized sectors of being as do other perceiving organs, are not permeable to personal acts which could alter them and change their significance.[64]

Those two aspects of the description are summed up, for Merleau-Ponty, in saying that perception belongs or adheres to a certain field, that it is given over, in the strongest sense of that phrase, to a certain perceptual field which it dominates—has the power to move around in—only inasmuch as it is already in complicity with it and already conscious of the laws that govern its being. The expressiveness of the sensible, consequently, is one with the expressiveness of the body. The interpenetration of the regions of being is one with that of the regions of the body. There is an intersensorial world in which color refers to sound, sound to color, texture to color, color to size and movement, because there is an intersensorial body in which the movements of the eye correspond to those of the hand and can be translated into them, not perfectly, but by undergoing a transformation into another system of equivalences. The corporeal schema explains in that manner the unity of the senses and the unity of the sensible thing.

With the notion of the corporeal schema, it is not only the unity of the body which is described in a new manner, it is also, through it, the unity of the senses and the unity of the object. My body is the place or rather the very actuality of the phenomenon of expression (*Ausdruck*), in it visual experience and auditive experience, for example, are pregnant with each other, and their expressive value grounds the prepredicative unity of the perceived world, and, by it, verbal expression (*Darstellung*) and intellectual signification (*Bedeutung*). My body is the common texture of all objects and it is, at least with respect to the perceived world, the general instrument of my "understanding." [65]

It is, perhaps, going too far and would be pushing this text beyond its own limits to say that the body is the world, but certainly it is Merleau-Ponty's intention to indicate that the body and the world have a common origin. The world is an expressive unity—in the sense of a system of equivalences—because the body is an expressive unity. And because they form two aspects of perceptual life, they are but two facets of the same sensible sense and presence. Yet, all the same, the sensible thing is a stranger to consciousness and, in fact, rejects the embrace of the body. The sensible thing in its individuality is not reducible to the gestures in which the body effects its exploration; it is alien and hostile. Nevertheless, it is the transcendence of the sensible which allows us to understand the primordial pact between the body and the world effected in perception and expressed for the *Phenomenology of Perception* in the notion of the corporeal schema. The familiarity of the body with the world is not to be explained by its relationship to what is given here and now in the field of perception. The body is a prepossession of the world as an operative intentionality, a habitual power to move along the lines suggested to it by the texture of things and by what is copresent in the background of the field. The movement from object to object in the perceptual field is achieved by capturing and realizing the general styles or sensible dimensions of the sensible: "A thing is, therefore, not actually *given* in perception, it is internally taken up by us, reconstituted and experienced by us in so far as it is bound up with a world, the basic structures of which we carry with us, and of which it is merely one of many possible concrete forms. Although a part of our living experience, it is nevertheless transcendent in relation to our life because the human body, with its habits which weave round it a human environment, has running through it a movement towards the world itself." [66]

As the operation of the body, perception does not start from things, but from the general structures of the world which correspond to its habitual potentiality for the world as a field of action. Perception comes to rest upon things and that leaves things with a sense of contingency and strangeness which is not overcome by the familiarity of the body with the general perceptual dimensions of the world. The general structures of the perceptual world—the universal texture of meaning—congeal, in the perception of individual things, in a specific event. Since it is from that universal texture that the individual event of perception takes its meaning and thus is accessible to the body, one and the same movement of perception can be an expression of the pact between the body and the world and an expression of the fact that in that pact the sensible thing eludes the grasp of the body and transcends the scope of human life.

Perception, consequently, is the belief in the world because it is a consciousness of the structure and general style of sensible things which corresponds to the general and anonymous life of the body. Passing from an illusion to real perception is a consciousness of having perceived first one sensible configuration and then another; an illusion is always what has been seen to lack reality. The sense of reality passes from one experience to the other without perceptual experience itself being reduced to an error or being thrown into doubt as a whole, for perception is the adherence of the body to a field. In perception one thing is replaced by another, because the perceptual field rearranges itself, a new configuration comes into being by means of a reshuffling of the tensions experienced in the illusion in the process of being canceled out. An illusion can be crossed out—there can be a transition from illusion to reality—because the general structures of perceptual being stand surety for the particular perceptual event. There is, Merleau-Ponty says, an absolute certitude about the world in general, but not about anything in particular. Truth is merely presumptive, since, because perception is always open to the world, each experience in its individuality does not *de jure* rule out other possibilities.[67]

The general format of the way in which the *Phenomenology of Perception* takes up the discussion of the expressive character of the body and of perception creates the dimensions of the question of language. The body is expression and the body speaks. For the discussion of physiognomic perception in the *Phenomenology of Perception,* the discovery of the expressive character of the perceiving body and of perception resulted from the particular manner in which perception expresses the sensible. And, consequently, the import of the phenomenology of perception for Merleau-Ponty lies not in the realm of psychology, for perception does not express what is internal to the psyche, but in the realm of ontology, for perception is a relationship to the Being of the sensible thing. The contours of the sensible thing and of sensibility are the contours of Being.[68] The discovery of the nature of expression in language follows the same route. Language, for Merleau-Ponty, is a relationship between the signifying and the signified and in a fundamental fashion between the spoken word and the world of perception.

In *The Structure of Behavior* the question of the relationship between language and the world of perception is framed in terms of the relationship between the mind and the body, while for the *Phenomenology of Perception* the question lies within the context of the expressive nature of the perceiving gesture. If the context within which language is discussed in the *Phenomenology of Perception* differs from that of *The Structure of Behavior,* that is not the only difference to be found between those two works in their treatment of language. For *The Structure of Behavior* the experience of others and the comprehension of intersubjective meaning is the work of language, and the problem of perception is how intersubjectively based meaning is perceived.[69] For the *Phenomenology of Perception* those dimensions of the experience of perception issue from the problematic of perception itself; perception is the expressive presence which brings into being the system of self, things, and others, and the physiognomic nature of perceptual meaning is such that it can sustain at its own level that tridimensional dispersion.[70] Yet the basic orientation of *The Structure of Behavior* with respect to the nature of language is one with that of the *Phenomenology of Perception* in seeing the original character of language in the operation of the authentic word—the expression of new meaning when language is one with thought.

In *The Structure of Behavior,* Merleau-Ponty writes that "the relations of the soul and the body can indeed be compared to those of concept and word, but on the condition of perceiving, beneath the separated products, the constituting operation which joins them and of rediscovering, beneath the empirical languages—the external accompaniment or contingent clothing of thought—the living *word* which is its unique actualization, in which the meaning is formulated for the first time and thus establishes itself as meaning and becomes available for later operations." [71] Nevertheless, *The Structure of Behavior* emphasizes the adherence of language to the intelligible world inasmuch as it is the *place* where intersubjective confrontations are situated and emphasizes the distance created by language between man and his immediate milieu to the extent that language creates a spectacle of that milieu and thus makes it the object of knowledge.[72] Along the same line of thought, there is for *The Structure of Behavior* clearly a physiognomy of perceptual meaning, but not so clearly a physiognomy of the thing, and hence the thing as an intersubjective reality rests, for *The Structure of Behavior,* more squarely on the nature of the *thing spoken* than on the accomplishments of perceptual behavior.[73]

The *Phenomenology of Perception* radicalizes the idea of original speech by deepening the sense of physiognomic perception and thus, as we have seen, clarifying the meaning of expression. The perspective gained by that discussion gives rise to an understanding of the being of language: language does not translate the being of things but the sense of perceptual existence. The perceiving body possesses its reality in being the symbol of existence and, therefore, in being the manner in which existence adheres to the world and is incorporated or inscribed into the being of the perceptual world. In the same manner language is the existence and symbol of thought; language is the expression of thought as the body is the expression of the totality of existence; language is the way that thought is in contact with things and hence open to the life-world.[74] That is what it means for words to *have* meaning.

Words have meaning as behavior has meaning, for the spoken word, for Merleau-Ponty, is veritable type of behavior and a true gesture: "The spoken word is a true gesture and contains its meaning as the gesture contains its." [75] For Merleau-Ponty, the concept of the word as gesture is not simply a heuristic device but the demarcation of the nature of the spoken word. There is a singular quality to linguistic meaning as there is a genuinely artistic style to the work of a painter and a specifically musical humor. Words exist within consciousness, not as positive contents of consciousness, but in the manner of the Freudian *Imago*—as a definite perceptual style. Words are retained in consciousness as acquisitions to fall back upon, not as points in logical space or as ideas enclosed in the repository of the unconscious, but as possible actions of the body, since they are first and foremost meaningful in their "articulatory and sonorous style." [76] Thus meaning is present within the word as it is present in an aesthetic work: by means of its perceptibility and because of its perceptibility.[77] It is, then, not going too far to speak of the word as a thing, in that the word, too, possesses a singular way of soliciting the movements of consciousness and awakening consciousness to the life of meaning, not by means of an idea, but by the way it is articulated in perception, by means of its perceptual style—its physiognomy.[78] "This incarnate sense," Merleau-Ponty writes, "is the central phenomenon with respect to which body and spirit, sign and signification are abstract moments." [79] As any gesture, therefore, the spoken word, in its internal articulation, configures its sense.

As a result, language does not signify meaning for Merleau-Ponty in the *Phenomenology of Perception* by pointing to the world; the source of its meaningfulness is not to be found in a reference to objects. Language does carry thought to the world, but only through its own gestural sense. In the *Phenomenology of Perception* Merleau-Ponty finds the original movement in language toward the world—the original contact between the world of perception and the spoken word—in the affective value of the meaning carried by the word. In its perceptual style the word captures an affective tonality in things, an existential signification inhabiting the world.[80] Language is not originally a representation of objects and of the relations between them. Such a consciousness or thought that thinks objects directly in and for themselves is grounded upon a more obscure thought. The language of clear and distinct ideas arises from a prior language whose model is not the logical activity of clarification, but the expression of things in their emotional essence. Words, consequently, are "so many ways of 'singing' the world." [81] And, since gestures and sentiments are invented, as are words, and not mere data, the task of language is not to make itself adequate to express the pregiven meaning of things. Rather, in what seems to be a paradox for a philosophy founded upon the primacy of perception as the original text of meaning, language in the final analysis speaks itself; it has its origins, not in the given world, but in the world according to man.[82]

Enrooted in the emergence of emotional gestures, language for Merleau-Ponty transcends the natural acts of the body to lend them a new significance. In language, the act of breathing becomes invested with a "figurative sense" which takes language outside of subjectivity toward the other and toward the thought of the subject himself.[83] Language is not only a system of constituted meanings—a repository of acquired expressions—but the *speaking* word (*parole parlante*): a "signifying intention which finds itself in the state of being born." [84] Operative language—a founding activity on a level with time, the fact, the unreflected, and perception [85]—encompasses two poles: constituted language (*parole parlée*), the system of expressions sedimented in speech, and constituting language (*parole parlante*), the speaking word which gives birth to expressed meaning.[86] The word, Merleau-Ponty states, "before becoming the symbol of a concept . . . is first of all an event which grips my body, and this grip circumscribes the area of significance to which it has reference." [87]

Just as the actual gestures of the body are incorporated into the life and the world of the body through the habituality—the habitual body—of its prepersonal hold upon the world, so the originality of the speaking word—constituting language—finds that the symbols to which it gives rise take on the being of the cultural world through constituted language. The transcendence of language toward new meaning can lay claim to being because of the way that meaning is sedimented and progressively acquired as the cultural world to which language habitually gives expression. The speaking word builds upon those acquisitions which live on within the cultural world, so that one can properly say that "the meaning of speech is nothing other than the way in which it handles this linguistic world or in which it plays variations on this keyboard of acquired meaning." [88] The world of language furnishes for the speaking word what nature on the level of the body furnishes for the natural gesture. In taking up the material supports provided for it within the sedimented acquisitions of its world and within the natural gestures of the body, language is natural and a nature. For it is inasmuch as the signs to which it gives rise are incorporated and inscribed into sensible being that language becomes the bearer of truth: the spoken word possesses a sense and opens up men to the possibility of truth because it is not a cry dissipated into the air once it has been uttered. Paradoxically, the cry lacks the density of being which would make it capable of signifying due to the fact that it uses the body as nature has given it. While, on the contrary, a poem possesses that density of being because it has been invented and thus rests more fully upon the power of expression; its meaning precipitates into the physiognomic sense of the speaking gesture. In that manner, the dialectic of language recapitulates at a different level the dialectic of the habitual and actual body in perception: existence creates a meaning beyond natural being and creates the word as "the empirical support of its own non-being." [89]

It is often overlooked that in the *Phenomenology of Perception* the experience which reveals the way that meaning inhabits language, the exact manner in which thought is bound to language, is the experience of the other. In hearing the language of the other, thought moves according to a progressive disclosure of meaning not of its own making. In following the inner articulations of his speech, we think according to the other and not according to ourselves. The other teaches us in the flow of his words what literally was not known beforehand. "There is then," in the words of Merleau-Ponty, "a taking up of the thought of the other across the spoken word, a reflection in the other, a power of thinking *according to the other* which enriches our own thoughts." [90] Thus the experience of the speech of the other is an experience of receiving an original signification in terms of which our thought is measured and provided with a norm. And, in addition, that measuring thought arises from the perceptibility of the speaking gestures which present it; it is literally heard and in that experience thought and hearing are indivisible. The experience of the language of the other is in that manner for Merleau-Ponty the experience of language in its starkest and hence most fundamental character. What the speaking and spoken word signifies is, therefore, an overt sense —open to the thought of others—and only grasped inasmuch as consciousness turns away from itself. In that sense, the experience of language is not a *cogitatio,* an act of consciousness, for its constituting principle lies not within self-consciousness, in consciousness as it is for itself, but in that prepersonal hold upon the world that is the original involvement of perception with the sensible.

Consciousness as the cogito is self-consciousness, the "I think" or self-apperception that accompanies all conscious acts and which gives to all the acts of consciousness their specific character of consciousness. As Derrida has shown in *Le voix et le phénomène,*[91] the paradigmatic experience of self-consciousness is the voice, the speaking act which hears itself and which, with Maine de Biran, is the apperception of itself in its own activity. Hearing oneself speak is thus to be conscious of oneself speaking and to be present to oneself. The voice is the presence of self to self and consequently the experience of the immanence of all meaning within consciousness, for in speaking to oneself—the voice—there is meaning inasmuch as it is enclosed within the relation of self to self. The paradigmatic experience of the voice as the original experience of meaning in consciousness is, then, also the foundation for the metaphysics of presence. Within the voice the being of the significations that words possess consists in the fact of their presence to consciousness, in the fact that they can be and are experienced within the relation of self to self—self-consciousness.

For self-consciousness and for the metaphysics of presence based upon self-consciousness, language is not originally communication. In the *Logical Investigations,*[92] the essence of expression, for Husserl, consists in the expression of the objective, logical meaning (*Bedeutung*) of the linguistic sign. And the linguistic sign expresses its sense inasmuch as it is animated by a meaning-bestowing act (*Bedeutungsintention*). The linguistic sign is directly the expression of the sense of the expressive act—the meaning-bestowing act, and only indirectly the manifestation of the psychic acts underlying the course of linguistic expression. For Husserl, the experience which reveals in its utmost clarity this structure of the linguistic sign is the experience of solitary discourse, for there the linguistic sign signifies its sense without manifesting psychic acts. Since in solitary discourse, consciousness as self-consciousness is manifest to itself—present to itself—the fact that the linguistic sign is meaningful rests, not upon its secondary role in manifesting feelings and emotions, but solely upon the objective meaning expressed in the sign. Communication is, from this vantage point upon the essence of language, not intrinsically involved in the structure of the linguistic sign. Communication is possible because the objective sense of the sign is ideal and hence distinct from the separate intentional acts that give it expression.

For Merleau-Ponty, on the contrary, the essence of expression lies in the structure of language disclosed in the experience of the language of the other. It is in the experience of communication that one learns by thinking according to the words of the other. The experience of that measure of one's own thought brings into focus the gestural nature of linguistic expression and that for the word to signify meaning is for it to be sonorous, a sensible physiognomy. Rather than shoring up the foundations of the philosophy of self-consciousness, the experience of language, as the *Phenomenology of Perception* elaborates it, places the nature of language at the level of the general and anonymous life of perception.

While that is clearly Merleau-Ponty's intention in the *Phenomenology of Perception* to look back from the vantage point provided by *Signs* and *The Visible and the Invisible,* the analysis of language in the *Phenomenology of Perception* fails to secure its own ground. The later works show a theoretical advance on two fronts. The first is the rejection of the idea of the silent cogito (*cogito tacite*) ; the second is the assimilation of the crucial import of the Saussurean conception of language. In the chapter on "the body as expression, and speech" Merleau-Ponty alludes to the Saussurean distinction between *langue and parole.*[93] Constituted language is identified with language as a system of signs (*langue*) ; constituting language is identified with speaking (*parole*), the individual act of communication. But while this distinction is explored and the opposition of the speaking word to the spoken word is essential for the analysis of language, yet one element in the Saussurean conception of the linguistic sign is absent: the diacritical nature of the sign. Consequently it is the physiognomic nature of the expressive gesture that provides the principal motif for the discussion of language and not the rapport of sign with sign which is crucial to Saussure's idea of language (*langue*). The assimilation of that perspective upon the structure of expression in language depends upon deepening the ties between language and perception. One barrier stands in the way of that task: the doctrine of the silent cogito. To cross that barrier is to engage the Saussurean distinction between *langue* and *parole* on the ground of the speaking word (*parole*) itself.

In one of the notes to *The Visible and the Invisible* dated February 1959, Merleau-Ponty states that if the opposition of *langue* to *parole* is the equivalent of the opposition of intersubjectivity to the individual, then the real nature of speaking is obscured, for "it is indeed the speaking, not the language [*la langue*] that aims at the other as a behavior, not as a 'psychism,' that responds to the other before he would have been understood as 'psychism,' in a confrontation that repels or accepts his utterances as utterances, as events—" [94] Intersubjectivity is the very subjectivity of the speaking word; it is not an individual act that utilizes an objective system of signs as a tool with which to carve out its own thought. The idea of language as a system of signs (*la langue*) presupposes that intersubjectivity, presupposes that the sense of the sign is transferable from individual to individual; it is not itself an original explanation of the activity of communication. Speaking is the experience of that presupposition, for as it "aims at the other as a behavior" it entails in its own structure the ability to exist on the same level with the other—it is as speaking an experience of the other. To understand speaking, it is necessary to install all that is meant by a system of signs (*langue*) in speaking itself. For Merleau-Ponty, rather than being opposed to speaking (*parole*), language as a system of signs belongs to the structure of the speaking act. "It is indeed," the note continues, "speaking that constitutes, *in front of* myself as a signification and a subject of signification, a milieu of communication, an intersubjective diacritical system which is the spoken tongue [*la langue*] in the present, not a 'human' universe, an objective spirit." [95]

The same note states why the silent cogito failed to come to terms with the intersubjectivity of the speaking word. More a problem itself than an explanation, the silent cogito prevents the relationship between language and perception from being posed in a fruitful manner. The silence that language finds in the world of perception does not leave language behind, for inasmuch as silence still retains a hold upon language it reveals the manner in which language and perception are part and parcel of the same being: the flesh. From the perspective of *The Visible and the Invisible* the silent cogito does not make comprehensible the passage from silent to spoken meaning, for to a world of sound it opposes a world of silence and thus, in absolving language of the silence that *Signs* discovers separating sign from sign, it makes it impossible to see that "the problem is grasp *what,* across the successive and simultaneous community of speaking subjects, *wishes, speaks,* and finally *thinks.*" [96]

In the *Phenomenology of Perception* itself the question of the silent cogito occurs in the context of the *cogito ergo sum* of Descartes's *Meditations.* The cogito with which Descartes wrote the *Meditations* and with which we read those *Meditations* is the spoken cogito and as such it is objective and general and not capable of revealing to us that active thinking or consciousness which "is engaged in fixing our life in conceptual forms, and thinking of it as indubitable." [97] In the spoken cogito the cogito is for itself the certainty of its own existence; in being objective and anonymous, the spoken cogito cannot itself be that intimate self-consciousness required as a starting point for Cartesian philosophy. That there is such a principle in spite of the general nature of the spoken cogito is due to the fact the cogito of the *Meditations* refers to a silent cogito that lives within me and is the relationship of my existence to itself. Unmediated by the acquisitions of the cultural world which intrude upon the spoken cogito, the silent cogito renders existence evident to itself in the indubitability of personal and individual existence.

But, if the spoken cogito refers to a silent cogito for Merleau-Ponty, it is not in the manner of a product related to the consciousness which produced it. The silent cogito is not a constituting consciousness, for language is not constituted by consciousness. Consequently the meaning of the silent cogito is formulated entirely within the limitations and within the context of language as *Fundierung,* an operative consciousness which lays down the dimensions of linguistic meaning as perception lays down the dimensions of perceptual meaning. The focus of the *Phenomenology of Perception* is on the way in which words take on their meaning by appealing to the motricity of the body and in realizing a sonorous style. For that reason, because its nature does not lie in positive, objective characteristics, language speaks meaning because it is taken up by "a consciousness of language, a silence of consciousness embracing the world of speech in which words first receive a form and meaning." [98] The reality of language does not consist in the existence of empirical languages or in constituted language, rather its reality encompasses the eruption of original and authentic speech. It involves an operating consciousness enrooted in individual consciousness, in the experience of self by self which, in being irreducible and not in full possession of itself, is the subjectivity at the basis of the creation of expressive language.

While the silent cogito is situated in the movements of authentic speech as the consciousness in which words take on expressive form and meaning, it, in turn, is bound by the nature of language. For "the tacit *cogito* is a *cogito* only when it has found expression for itself." [99] It is in itself only an experience of self that arises in extreme situations such as the imminence of death. Thus it does not exist in an explicit manner for itself, but exists more like an inarticulate grip upon the being of the world, almost a raw claim upon the right to existence. To be for itself the silent cogito must avail itself of the means of expression; it is only through words that it can think itself and become self-consciousness. The subjectivity that in the silent cogito precedes language is not, then, a subjectivity that posits itself, nor objective thought, but a primordial subjectivity whose confused, open, and indefinite unity corresponds to the ambiguous unity of the world. In the final analysis, the silent cogito is not a self-consciousness, but a sense of belonging to oneself as "one single experience," "a living cohesion," and a "single temporality."

It would seem, then, that the possibility of the transference of sense—expression—and the communication of meaning from the world of perception to the cultural world of language lies in there being a consciousness of language that as a silent cogito has roots in the silent world of perception. Expression would be possible because there exists a consciousness of language operating prior to language yet part of it, since it is situated not in constituted language but in constituting language, authentic speech. The language which originally moves from silence to sound reveals a cogito different from the spoken cogito accessible to all, an irreducible cogito—irreducible because it belongs to itself and is responsible for the uniqueness of individual existence. The transference of sense—expression—from the silent world of perception to the spoken world of expressed meaning in the *Phenomenology of Perception* is made possible by a consciousness of language which adheres to itself and thus affirms an independence from the constituted world of the spoken cogito. In touch with the unique dimensions of existence, it is that consciousness that leads language into the expression of what has not been said before. The silent cogito is the consciousness that forms the very movement from perception to language—the pathway along which perceptual sense travels in unfolding itself in the world of expressions. Within the speaking word, the expressive life of corporeal subjectivity is mediated by a consciousness which, in its silence, still retains a hold upon the mute world of perception.

An essay in *Sense and Non-Sense,* "The Metaphysical in Man," dating from the same year as the *Phenomenology of Perception,* locates the contribution of Saussure's linguistics in the view that rejecting a causal explanation of language sees language as a totality. In a manner comparable to the way Gestalt psychology discovered the being of the perceptual object, linguistics through the idea of structure discovers language to possess a being which is neither objective nor subjective, in fact a being beyond those alternatives. Inasmuch as language possesses as a totality an internal logic of its own, linguistic facts are mediated by consciousness without consciousness being the milieu of language. In that internal logic there is revealed an operative life (*vie operante*), a project that is one with language itself, its life within speaking subjectivity. This discovery of an operative life within language is, as was the case for the *Phenomenology of Perception,* the disclosure of the manner in which language is the signifying life of speaking subjectivity. Language is a preconscious intentionality that the speaker must assume in order for the desire to speak to find a place in the intersubjective world of culture.[100] "Language," Merleau-Ponty writes, "must *surround* each speaking subject, like an instrument with its own inertia, its own demands, constraints, and internal logic, and must nevertheless remain open to the initiative of the subject (as well as to the brute contributions of invasions, fashions, and historical events), always capable of the displacement of meanings, the ambiguities, and the functional substitutions which give this logic its lurching gait." [101]

To view language as a totality is still, however, to be on the threshold of Saussure's conception of language. Yet what is decisive is that the perspective upon language achieved by the *Phenomenology of Perception* corresponds to the experience of language in structural linguistics. And linguistics joins from its side the experience of language emanating from the phenomenological analysis of perception. That juncture indicates the route that Merleau-Ponty's reflections upon the being of language will take, not for accidental reasons, but for intrinsic reasons. For linguistics itself discloses, through its own understanding of language, the essential dimensions of the speaking word. And Saussure's conception of language introduces a further step in those reflections, a step that introduces what is specific to the rejection of the silent cogito and, at the same time, what is essential to the capture of the intersubjective nature of language and to the comprehension of the way in which the sign signifies. In *The Visible and the Invisible* those two sides of the question of language find common expresssion in the characterization of language as an "intersubjective diacritical system." The interrogation of the diacritical nature of the sign in Saussure's linguistics introduces, consequently, that further step which prolongs and deepens for Merleau-Ponty the question of language.

The diacritical nature of the sign is introduced in a course Merleau-Ponty taught at the Sorbonne in 1949–50. There Merleau-Ponty said: "Saussure admits that language *(langue)* is essentially diacritical: words bear a meaning much less than they put some other words at a distance from themselves. That amounts to saying that every linguistic phenomenon is a differentiation of a global movement of communication. In a language *(langue)*, Saussure says, everything is negative, there are only differences without positive terms. The signified side reduces itself to conceptual differences; the signifying side to phonetic differences." [102] The approach to the relationship between expression and the expressed, the sign and its meaning, lies along the course charted by the differential or diacritical nature of the sign. Meaning in language, rather than being a positive element, is a relation. And, more strongly, it is a relation only revealed across a backdrop of negativity: the differences between signs. The sign expresses a meaning—and hence is both a sense and a consciousness—that spans the distances that language interposes between words. As a speaking word, language is the totality arising from those differences, a differential system and not a preordained logical order.

It is in that way that Merleau-Ponty can view the theoretical efforts of Saussure in linguistics as expressing the perspective of spoken language and that of the speaking subject who is "completely the will to be understood and to understand." [103] For inasmuch as language is a differential system, an ordering of interrelations between its elements, it makes it possible to see how spoken language is not the sensible covering for a constituted thought, but the movement of differences in which meaning is expressed. Thus the differential character of speaking subjectivity reveals as its very mode of being the conjuncture of the individual act of speaking and the system of signs making that speaking a signifying process. To speak is already to possess the possibility of being understood, for each individual expression is a modulation of the system of differences and divergences in which the sign reveals its sense.

Joined to those considerations, which are important for the development of Merleau-Ponty's involvement with the question of language, is a line of thought whose import only appears clearly in *La prose du monde* and in *Signs*. At the same time that Saussure's thought deepens the significance of the experience of language for Merleau-Ponty, it also provides an access to the nature of history. For Merleau-Ponty in *The Visible and the Invisible, Signs,* and *La prose du monde* the diacritical nature of language and aesthetic perception provide the basis for the understanding of history. In the course of 1949–50 on language Merleau-Ponty writes that "the principle of historical order and rationality turn, as Saussure almost said, the fortuitous into systems." [104] History and language possess, if not a common rationality, at least common dimensions such that the structure of the sign poses questions that are also at the heart of the structure of history: those that bear upon the rationality arising from the event of meaning in perception. Language and history both involve the same intersubjectivity, for speaking subjectivity aims directly at the behavior of the other and consists in the desire to be understood and "what moves every historical development is the common situation of men, their will to coexist and to recognize each other." [105] As Merleau-Ponty affirms in *La prose du monde,* this mediation effected between event and system is the unique perspective that Saussurean linguistics introduces into the comprehension of the rationality of history: "In any case, Saussure has the great merit of taking the step which liberates history from historicism and makes possible a new conception of reason." [106]

La prose du monde, in reviewing language as an internal logic elaborated through the differences separating sign from sign and thus creating what is proper to linguistic expression, joins with *Humanism and Terror* in placing the rationality of history upon the basis of the event. For the phenomenology of language, it is a logic immersed in its events which characterizes the sensible existence of language. Although Saussure himself tended to oppose the synchronic view of language to the diachronic view, for Merleau-Ponty, nevertheless, they converge and overlap to form the specific being of language. For the sign is an event signifying through its relations with other signs and hence in its very fortuitous nature in terms of an expressive system, a logic, a way of modulating meaning that is not the spiritual existence of thought, but the inherent organization of sensibility. Significantly for Merleau-Ponty it is the phenomenology of language that places in question the phenomenology of Husserl, for it is clearly not as a positional or thetic act that the sign signifies for Merleau-Ponty, but as diacritical: signs allude to their significations. And it is that allusive character—which creates an indirect language—which highlights the way in which expressed meaning inheres in the sensible, corporeal nature of the sign and makes of language a "corporeal intentionality." [107]

From this perspective, the essay in *Signs,* "On the Phenomenology of Language," describes the sense present in the spoken word as a trace. Meaning is not inherent to the speaking gesture as a sense posited by an act of consciousness. The sense spoken by language is not a positive content held captive and circumscribed by the sign; it is, on the contrary, a relation between signs which resides in the "texture of the linguistic gesture." And hence the diacritical nature of the sign exposes a relationship between the signifying and the signified that places the center of expression elsewhere than in the rapport of language and thought. The expressive nature of language does not lie in the lateral relationship of thought and language — words do not express already explicit ideas — but in the lateral relations existing between words.

The signifying intention which gives rise to expression and which one usually associates with the movements of conscious thought is not a movement on a level other than that of words, but a "gap" — an absence of sense felt in what has already been said and what demands to be spoken — whose only adequate response to what it wants to say consists in speaking. On the level of significations, the task of language is never finished and expression is consequently never total. What is aimed at in speaking and what is expressed in words are not given before language, but are poles or vortices around which expressions cluster to merge into a signifying effort. Expression is achieved, then, when in and through the systematic relations constituting language there arises a new signification whose sense lies in being a new variation upon the rapports already established between signs and their significations. It is in this act of modulation and variation that Merleau-Ponty finds the specific nature of expression in language. Expression does not consist in an act that *ex nihilo* launches a new meaning into the cultural world; rather, it consists in a spread of sense created by the contrast and opposition between the past and present arrangement of signifying elements.

The act of expression thus is specifically a decentering of language, a reorganization of the axes along which significations move which creates the space in which what has not been said before can install itself. The basis of expression in language is a "coherent deformation" effected in language by the intentions constituting it: "It is just this 'coherent deformation' (Malraux) of available signification which arranges them in a new sense and takes not only the hearers *but the speaking subject as well through a decisive step.*" [108] Expression is also the sedimentation of significations in the ensemble of existing significations, for once expressed, meaning becomes incorporated into the total sense of the cultural world. In its transcendence—the signifying intention—and in its sedimentation, the speaking word is sustained as expression and rendered actual by the fact that the sense it speaks lies across the distances separating words and becomes expression in varying those distances in such a way that it can appear.

To speak, therefore, is not an act of creation, but one of re-creation; it is to seek an equivalent within the system of significations open to the signifying intention and to realize a definite reorganization in the system. But expression is not summed up in the description of the signifying intention. The essence of expression for Merleau-Ponty also lies in another direction: in the surpassing of the signifying by the signified. Captured across the differences between signs and not contained within them, meaning is born in signs as a trace, a silent testimony to the passage of the signifying intention. Significations are not positive givens, but perpetually absent originals signified by the gestures which bear their imprint.

Moreover, expression is a corporeal intentionality, an intentionality of those speaking gestures which trace in their physiognomy the significations they allude to, and, as a consequence, trace in their features the incorporation of the signifying intention: the stabilization of that deformation in new formations. The incorporation of meaning into the cultural world, underscored by the process of sedimentation, is the other side of the transcendence of the signifying gesture and makes possible the originality of expression by embedding it in the social and cultural patterns of the world.

"Indirect Languages and the Voices of Silence," the essay in *Signs* which issued from the revision of the manuscript, *La prose du monde,* reaffirms those ideas on language and encloses them in a larger, ultimately more significant context. For since both works are a reflection on language mediated by an analysis of mute expression in painting, they reveal the specific problematic of the question of language for the later thought of Merleau-Ponty. In prolonging the consciousness of the world found in perception, language draws in its wake the question of history and through that question the question of the ultimate nature of being. For if it is true that Mer-

leau-Ponty locates the place where Husserlian phenomenology is
thrown into question in the phenomenology of language, then it is
also true to say that it is through language that the being proper to
the perceptual world is rediscovered and its impact properly continued. Because of the diacritical nature of the sign, language is a
certain interiority; it is a totality of relations signifying across the
spread of signs and thus a totality, like the sensible thing, sensitive
to itself and issuing from the internal rapports constituting it. But
to thus locate meaning in language at the edges of signs and not in
their centers is to also show how meaning is sedimentated in language
and has an intrinsic adherence to history. It is placing meaning
within a "symbolic context" that dates it, that gives it the imprint
of a definite historical present and ties its sense to that specific
present.[109]

Because the meaning of the sign is entirely within language, at
the intersections of linguistic gestures, language has an autonomy
and an opaqueness that makes it more than a means for thought.
The specific inherence of meaning in the junctures of signs makes it
a *kind of being.* Consisting solely in the convolutions and invo-
lutions of the relations between signs, language in a way is a reference to itself; it folds back upon itself to give it a general reflexivity
—or reversibility in the language of *The Visible and the Invisible*—
bearing no claim to the title of self-consciousness. But, then, the being that language reveals is one that matches its relationship to
meaning. Itself not sound, but the relations forming the matrix of
sounds and the space of their dispersion into individual signs, language for Merleau-Ponty is indirect, allusive, and ultimately silence.
Neither originally the embodiment of thought in sound, nor the
reference of signs to things, language carries meaning from sign to
sign across relations and distances that themselves are not spoken,
but are originally the silence which sensible gestures must traverse
into order to gain a hold upon expression. "Language," Merleau-
Ponty writes, "bears the meaning of thought as a footprint signifies
the movement and effort of a body." [110] The sign is a trace of the
movement toward expression; in its gestural sensibility it speaks a
sense that spanning each individual sound is ultimately heard in
silence.

In saying that "we would undoubtedly recover the concept of history in the true sense of the term if we were to get used to modeling it after the example of the arts and language," Merleau-Ponty intends to indicate that the truth of history lies in the same struggle that language takes up for expression and the institution of meaning in the cultural world.[111] It involves the same encroachment of transcendence upon the sedimentation of events into the acquisitions of the past. And hence the truth which history captures as the work of man appears across the excess of the present over the past.[112] The event of expression as well as the historical event — inasmuch as it launches a new direction to be explored — is not a meaning enclosed in a hermetically sealed present. Emerging from the variations they effect upon the sedimented significations of the past, both can be understood exactly as a passage toward expression, one in words, the other in actions. The truth spoken in language is thus in its intimate bonds with the rationality of history a truth tied down to its divergence from the past which it holds in its wake; and the truth realized in history is a truth lived through the efforts men make to live the contours of their present against the background of past institutions and culture.

The preface to *Signs* extends the direction of those reflections on the Being of language. There Merleau-Ponty introduces the question of language in the context of the reflection carried to the point of infinity that is involved when eyes meet. As glances crisscross each other and give rise to the situation: I see you seeing me seeing you . . . one ego is created. The spoken word breaks that fascination, but does not obliterate it; it carries it further and articulates it and, in that way, extends within the folds of language the pathways from the self to the other forming silent communication.[113] In addition, extending the hold that perception has upon the silent and mute world of things, the speaking word also elaborates, on the level of symbols, the silent communication that is part and parcel of the intercorporeity manifested in the experience of gaze penetrating gaze and hand touching hand. Vision and touch are already communication and already live an intersubjectivity which language does not create, but, as a corporeal gesture, assumes and turns in a different direction.

The language that Merleau-Ponty is speaking of is the operative word which charts beforehand the course that thought must take in coming to expression. Thought crawls along in language; that is the way it is put elsewhere. The preface to *Signs* says, "the operative word makes us think and live thought magically finds its words." [114] From the viewpoint of expression, the relevant distinction is not, then, between thought and language, but between successful expression—thought—and aborted expression—language. It is only when words fail to fulfill their own intentions that one notices them, that they are obstacles to what one wants to say. That experience is properly the experience of language as a totality of means for expression distinct from thought. The speaking, operative word is thought itself on the move, seeking out the essences of things and reaching out for the words of the other. Hence expressive operations pass from the thinking word to the speaking word and not from thought to language. The movement of expression is totally encompassed within the intentions and structure of language itself; symbols, as Pierce said, grow out of symbols. Thoughts, far from being spiritual entities, are for operative language—thought on the move in words—"open totalities of available significations"; directions which in being indicated by words yet remain open to be explored. The sign as a divergence between signs signifies the manner in which thought is formed in the breaks and intersections forming the course of language from sign to sign. Thought in language is intersticial.

In language is to be found a movement toward expression that, passing through the anonymous hold of the sign upon signification, is already installed in a world of nameable things and arises from an uneasiness in things themselves which calls for expression.[115] Inasmuch as language varies and amplifies intercorporeal communication, it is already in rapport with things and with the sensible world that is traversed by the eye and the hand. The perceptual world is a layer of meaning irreducible to the expressions of language, but nonetheless intimately connected with the latter, for what separates those two layers—perception and language—is not different meanings to be given to things—the percept and the concept—but two different ways of elaborating the same sense of things.

Hence perception and language communicate with one another; the sense of things is transferred from one layer of meaning to the other, not through a change in being, but through a "coherent deformation" in which what is perceived finds its equivalent in another physiognomic configuration. The passage from one to the other lies along the strands which unite, within the intersensorial body, visibility to tangibility and language to perception. Things are already spoken because we have a body and because that body speaks: "Thus things *find themselves spoken* and *thought* as if by a Word (*Parole*) and by a Thinker which we do not possess, but which possesses us." [116]

The interrogation of the Being of language, as well as the interrogation of the Being of the perceived world, raises the question of what speaks in language and what sees and touches in vision and touch. The Being of the sensible inhabits the body and the words which find expression in corporeal gestures. Surrounding the visible thing is the tissue of perceptual dimensions, lines, shadows, colors, etc., that, while not seen themselves and hence invisible, *make things visible*. Surrounding the perceptibility of words, in the tissue of their sensibility, are the differentiations and divergences separating sign from sign which mark the passage of meaning through signs. Just as, then, the being of visibility and tangibility is woven from the relation of what is visible to its horizon of invisibility penetrating it, so language possesses a dimension of invisibility—thought —revealed in the silence accompanying the traces of meaning in speech. Things are visible inasmuch as their visibility opens onto an invisibility; words signify inasmuch as they open onto a silence inhabiting them.

We are brought, in that fashion, to the threshold of *The Visible and the Invisible*. By revealing an interiority in the passage of meaning across the continual traversing of the distances between signs constituting the speaking word, the interrogation of Saussurean linguistics brings the philosophy of language before the presence of a word in which expression is already bound to things and in which things are already spoken. One confronts in language, as in perception, a savage Being in terms of which and at whose level philosophy as the philosophy of consciousness becomes irrelevant.[117] The ultimate Being of language is to be found in that wild and untamed spirit or thought lurking beneath the commonplace sound of words and beneath the familiarity with which we usually treat them. We speak by lending ourselves to a thought in language that, through the divergences of signs and through the words of others which create in us "a divergence in relation to . . ." speaks in us. The silence of language is not that of a silent cogito, but the silence of the thought in language which makes us hear as it makes us speak.[118]

One is clearly misled, consequently, in seeing in the thought of *The Visible and the Invisible*—the interrogation of the wild Being of language, its *flesh*—suggestions of the later writings of Heidegger on language and Being. In a note dated September 1959, Merleau-Ponty writes: "the Saussurean analysis of the relations between signifiers and the relations from signifier to signified and between the significations (as differences between significations) confirms and rediscovers the idea of perception as a *divergence (écart)* by relation to a *level,* that is, the idea of the primordial Being, of the Convention of conventions, of the speech before speech." [119] This philosophy which finds the thought operative in the differences constituting meaning in language to be the expression of the savage Being of language is a thought immersed in the passage of sense through the speaking word. Aiming at the behavior of the other, language is an operative word spanning the experience of the other and stemming from the challenge that the mute presence of things presents to expression. The Being of language arises in the folds of that system of "Self-World-Others" first revealed in the overture to the world in physiognomic perception. Its Being is that of the flesh; the Being of things and the Being of language disclose, across the intercourse of perception and sensible things and the intercourse between men, a world of untamed unconquerable meaning.

The Visible and the Invisible is only a truncated philosophy of language. It ends at the point where the problematic of intersubjectivity is introduced and hence at the very juncture where the preface to *Signs* introduces language. *The Visible and the Invisible,* in the incomplete form in which we have it, is only an introduction to language from the perspective of the philosophy of the flesh. *The Visible and the Invisible* once again turns to language to interrogate its sense and in that way to reexperience language. Much more than a concept, the flesh is the experience of language lived through interrogative discourse, a question that re-creates the presence of the questioned. The experience of language is the experience of a truth lived in the thick and embroiling relations we have with others, in the ideas presented in conversations that grope for a center which often eludes them and are more the expression of the emotions in which they are embedded than indications of the cool judgments they often pretend to represent.[120] Our contact with ideas in language is thus an experience of a "savage thought."

In the thickness and opacity of words, language is an extension of the relations which the body has with the sensible world and those it has with the bodies of others. It is clearly in the experience of raw meaning—in love, in anger, in despair, in joy—"a relation to Being through a being, and like it, it is narcissistic, eroticized, endowed with a natural magic that attracts the other significations into its web, as the body feels the world in feeling itself."[121] In its relationship to ideas, language *in practice*—the language of life, action, literature, and poetry—recapitulates the relationship of the body to the world. Language involves a reflexivity or reversibility found in the hand[122] touching hand and, in the same reversibility found there—one hand is touching, then touched—it involves a relationship to ideas as the invisible dimension of silence. The comparison of the operations of the body with the operative life of language is, consequently, more than an analogy. It is a strict explanatory principle in which the Being of language can be comprehended.

Held captive by the meanings born of its expressions rather than holding them captive, language speaks *according to* meaning, as in the experience of the language of the other, one thinks *according to* the words of the other. Thought is not the birth of meaning, but the birth, the eruption of meaning within language is thought. Speaking within the divergences that constitute the space between signs and the space between the speaker and the other is to speak within a Speaking Word that contains the speaker and those who hear him: "No one thinks anymore, everyone speaks, all live and gesticulate within Being."[123] Called forth by the surfeit of meaning in the sensible world—the invisible—language in its relationship to meaning and in its relationship to visible and tangible being "lives only from silence." [124] It is caught up in a reversibility and corporeal bond with the perceptual world that forms the tissue and texture of its audible signs. It too as the silent life of ideas has the very Being of the sensible, the flesh; its Being is that of a "porous Being," of a Being with folds, for as the Being of the incarnate, being is at once dispersed and gathered between the body and the world.

And it is through the flesh of language that thought is inserted in the world of perception. The mediation that effects the transition from the mute presence of things to the articulations of expression follows the articulations of the flesh itself. As a sensible thing sensible to itself—a vision seeing itself, a touch touching itself—the body has a twofold Being that places it at once among sensible beings as one of them and on the other side of them as what is not seen or touched, but the seeing and the touching. Sensible things, as seen from the outside, as the body too sees itself from the outside, are the doubles of the body; they too have an invisible side *according to* which the visible and the tangible erupt before the eye and under the hand. There is a flesh, then, of the world because the world possesses a relationship to the body that recapitulates the body's relationship to itself—its reversibility—in being a sensible seeing and a sensible seen, a sensible touching and a sensible touched. The flesh is this intertwining and redoubling that unites visibility and tangibility and the body and the world. "The body," Merleau-Ponty writes in *The Visible and the Invisible,* "unites us directly with the things through its own ontogenesis, by welding to one another the two outlines of which it is made, its two laps: the sensible mass it is and the mass of the sensible wherein it is born by segregation and upon which, as seer, it remains open." [125] In their sonorous Being, linguistic gestures are inscribed into this reversibility of the flesh. The reflexivity of language is the doubling of speaking and hearing at the same time that it is the relation of the audible to silence. Part of the sensible itself, language as an operative life articulates its expressions in terms of the Being of that sensible thing which is also an expressive life, the body. Language adheres to the world as flesh; thought only occurs to one that is flesh.

The reversibility found in the voice, in the doubling of speech and hearing, does not, however, in *The Visible and the Invisible* serve as a paradigm for the nature of reflection. I do not hear myself as others hear me; similarly the hand touched and the hand touching do not exactly coincide, rather they anticipate one another; they are an encroachment upon one another rather than a coincidence. Only for a philosophy of coincidence would that experience signify failure; and only if it were a success would consciousness be self-consciousness. The two sides of speaking do not coincide, nor do the two sides of the body, because they are spanned by the total Being of the body and of the world.[126] The failure of the body or language to coincide with themselves exposes to view the texture of the flesh, the specific rapport of visibility to invisibility and of sound to silence. It is that relation that makes the body sensitive to itself and thus flesh; it is that same relation that creates in language the carnal presence of ideas.

Ideas owe their existence and the power of their impact to that carnal presence, "to the fact," Merleau-Ponty says, "that they are in transparency behind the sensible, or in its heart." [127] As a level or dimension of sensibility and not distinct from it as another kind of being, the existence of sense in language is dependent upon the reversibility of the flesh. And as such, ideas create the ideality of the flesh itself as its axes, depths, and dimensions. The operation of the flesh in language is found in the way that the sense of the sign reflects back upon the arrangement of the sounds which mark the progress of its realization and comprehension. Once realized it casts its shadow back over them as they recede into the past to become their sense, the meaning they have expressed. Because of that reversibility or retrograde action words bear meaning.[128] The presence of ideas in language bears witness to the existence of the flesh: "their carnal texture presents to us what is absent from all flesh; it is a furrow that traces itself out magically under our eyes without a tracer, a certain hollow, a certain interior, a certain absence. . . ." [129]

The foundation of the signifying power of language for *The Visible and the Invisible* is, therefore, the dehiscence or eruption of the flesh within language. The reflection of signification back upon the audible signs expressing it, the generosity of language which moves thought immediately to the expressive sense of things, the reversibility of the sign and its differential character, all testify to the fact that language has a life of its own, a silent life. As the trace of the silent armature of thought, of the carnal presence of ideas, and of the invisible, in being flesh language speaks the Being of the world. Secondly, it is silence that sustains for Merleau-Ponty in *The Visible and the Invisible* the movements of language as the invisible sustains the transitions between touching and seeing and, in general, the reversibility of the flesh. Thirdly, language possesses man, not as its instrument, but through the intersubjectivity and generality of the flesh. Operative language is at once a rapport with self, others, and the sensible world. Language speaks out of silence, as the laying down of the horizon of invisibility—thought—and as an opening up and installation of itself in that horizon as an anticipation and for-having (*Vorhabe*) of the nameable. The thought of language takes place in the divergences of words, in the divergence of the self from others, and in its reversibility, in the divergence of language from itself. Language possesses consciousness, because consciousness is in the grips of the world and open to others: in the folds of the flesh.

And thus we have come full cycle. The "hyperreflection" that *The Visible and the Invisible* sees as issuing from the demands that in-terrogative language places upon philosophy [130] is a discourse that structures itself around the indirect expression of Being. The inter-rogative style of philosophical thought is the way that language itself lives its rapport with the flesh of the world: within its folds. Inter-rogation is hence a style of thought expressed in the structure of discourse. Inseparable from the texture in which they silently move, the ideas to which that interrogative thought gives expression are tied inseparably to the vagaries and detours of that language. Trans-forming itself into a literary text, philosophy expresses the sense of the world by creating, through the differences and divergences mark-ing the route of expressions, a space and a time in which and along which the experience of the raw and stark Being of the sensible world may be relived. Or perhaps it is only in that space and time that the sense of the world is lived for the first time. For philosophy does not create the space and time of expression; it assumes them in order to leave on them the imprint of its own intentions. Language is, already, the expression of the world. And the question of philoso-phy is, then, the question for philosophy: how to coexist with the struggle proper to expression; how to be language.

2

Don Ihde

SINGING THE WORLD
LANGUAGE AND PERCEPTION

PHENOMENOLOGY is a revolution in man's understanding of himself and his world. But the newness and radicality of this revolution is faced with a problem, the same problem which arises in the epiphany of any new phenomenon. What phenomenology has to say must be made understandable—but what it has to say is such that it cannot be said easily in a language already sedimented and accommodated to a perspective quite different from that taken by the revolutionary. What eventually may be said must first be "sung." One only gradually learns to hear what sounds forth from the "song."

Not long ago an illustrative event of like dimensions occurred when the "songs" of whales were recorded. The listener, in every case known to me, would first be taken aback by the strangeness, the mysterious, enchanting, uncanny quality of the songs. Fascinated and even awed by this new language from the sea, deep stirrings of feeling occurred. Then a second phase of appropriation would begin through associations and metaphors: "That's *like* a bull bellowing," "It's *like* electronic music," "2001," "Now I can see how the legends of the sirens began." Here the listener attempts to relate the uncanny to something which is already familiar—and that's as far as most go. With the mysterious partly domesticated one is satisfied. But a further thought is possible: this is, after all, neither siren, nor electronic music, nor bull—it *is* the humpback whale sounding forth, "singing the world" in his own way. It is for us to listen, to enter that strange song as best we can if we are to discern the contours of that world. For this, more than curiosity is called for. The whale song issues a call to whose resonances we cannot yet fully respond.

Language, "singing the world," is a philosophical problem. But that problem is more acute for the phenomenologist. The phenomenologist, faced with ordinary language filled with the sediments of a past history, must learn to sing in a new way. Merleau-Ponty was quite aware of the difficulties of both saying and hearing something new in his struggle to express himself. Of philosophies he said, "I begin to understand a philosophy by feeling my way into its existential manner, by reproducing the tone and accent of the philosopher. In fact, every language conveys its own teaching and carries its meaning into the listener's mind." [1]

I want to focus the question of language as the foreground of this essay on Merleau-Ponty because language is one, if not *the* Archimedian point from which other questions may be levered from their dominance in the background of thought. Behind, under, eventually beyond spoken language lies the world of perceived, wild being which is Merleau-Ponty's more apparent focus. For him it is through the question of perception that the question of language and expression is reached, but it is through the question of language that the enigmas of perception may also be seen.

Nor are the questions of language and perception separable for Merleau-Ponty. Phenomenologically the world is already primitively given as meaningful in some sense. There is no pure datum, no raw qualia or pure sense from which to begin; rather, man begins immersed in a world already significant, already both "natural" and "cultural," and the phenomena of immersion are the first to be interrogated. Thus if I begin by reversing Merleau-Ponty's emphasis it is because that reversal is suggested by his work itself. Insofar as perception and expression remain paired it is possible to begin from either side of the pairing, noting, of course, that a reversal of order may also reveal aspects not apparent from the other side.

The initial practical problem—how does one make phenomenology understandable?—is at base more profoundly philosophical. It is too easy for the philosopher already assuming and inhabiting the "phenomenological attitude" to hold that the problem is not one of language at all. Nor is it, if all problems of language are those of particular propositions or of logics and grammars. The problem is one of a shift in stance. Once one learns to "see" as a phenomenologist, then what has been said by Husserl, Heidegger, and Merleau-Ponty appears neither obscure nor ambiguous. The problem is one of attaining a perspective, not one of uttering a correct formula. But this shift of perspective *is* a problem of language in a deeper sense. In elaborating the nonneutral, embodied theory of language in the *Phenomenology of Perception,* Merleau-Ponty noted that language "presents or rather it *is* the subject's taking up of a position in the world of his meanings." [2]

In this preliminary sense phenomenology, too, is the taking up of a position in the world of philosophical meanings. It, too, is situated as a focus within Being. It, too, "sings the world" in its own style. And our task is to listen to that song.

I shall attempt first to develop some of the characteristic marks of Merleau-Ponty's notion of language. By situating his work in the context of a philosophical tradition and noting some features of the growth of a radical language, by outlining the distinctive features of an explicit theory of language, and then by noting the role language plays vis-à-vis perception, I hope to show the justification for this reversal of emphases.

In the preface to *Phenomenology of Perception,* Merleau-Ponty explicitly situates his work in the context of the phenomenological philosophy issued earlier from Husserl. Merleau-Ponty sees his own development of phenomenology as a nuanced divergence from certain aspects of Husserlianism. First, the perceptual world is primary, the base from which one must begin and the primitive field which must be thoroughly explored. Second, the examination of this field will yield certain essential ambiguities about man and his relations to his world which are revealed better by a focus upon the *genesis* of meaning than by attaining a description of stable essences. And, third, the genetic emphasis will result in the development of an *existential* as contrasted with a transcendental idealist philosophy.

In situating himself alongside Husserl, Merleau-Ponty also adapts and refines a strategy used earlier by Husserl. The *Phenomenology of Perception* employs a polemic against both empiricist and rationalist traditions, against their mechanist and intellectualist outcomes. Posed positively against these traditions is the emergent existentialist philosophy developed by Merleau-Ponty. This positive position belongs to that class of contemporary anti-Cartesian philosophies which reject the dualism of mechanical, material extended substance and psychological, subjective mental substance. In contrast, Merleau-Ponty's existential position elaborates a unitary theory of embodied being.

But taking a polemic position is taking a position within an already constituted world of philosophical meanings. There is a price to be paid: not only must the existentialist position which emerges be drawn in contrast to dominant philosophies, it must also first address itself to its opponents in the very language of those opponents. If Cartesianism is to be rejected, what replaces it? If sense data are rejected, what is perception? The form of the questions resituates us in the midst of a linguistic problem. If there is to be a new framework and a new language to express the insights appropriate to an existential phenomenological position, how are those expressions to emerge from the nonneutral philosophical past?

Three degrees of increasingly radical language uses are discernible: a) one seeks to use standard terms and gradually change their meanings, one adapts them to new usages; b) one creates new terms (neologisms, compound words) and employs metaphors to infuse new meaning; c) and one borrows words from other contexts not previously used by philosophers. (One might add, that the result (d) would be an extension in which the new language will be a new technical vocabulary as the new tradition itself begins to resediment after the stirring it initially caused.) Merleau-Ponty utilizes all three of these levels, but in varying stages.

a) Early the tendency is to be more conservative. *The Structure of Behavior* attempts to infuse Gestalt terminology with a nascent phenomenology. Within the polemic structure of the *Phenomenology of Perception* the standard terms are again reworked. Indeed, key philosophical terms are often dealt with in the manner of (a), but filled with new meaning. *Perception* is a significant sample. Perception is primary for Merleau-Ponty, but perception becomes both broader and more inclusive than its previous philosophical use. His defense of the thesis of the primacy of perception before the Société Française de Philosophie is an attempt to widen the very meaning of perception.

By these words, "the primacy of perception," we mean that the experience of perception is our presence at the moment when things, truths, values are constituted for us; that perception is a nascent logos; that it teaches us, outside all dogmatism, the true conditions of objectivity itself; that it summons us to the tasks of knowledge and action.[3]

Here *perception* must carry a load seldom imposed upon it by philosophy since its equivalent in the pre-Socratics.

    b) Similar adaptations and transformations happen with *subject, thinking, imagination, object*. But the essentially conservative strategy of importing new meanings to old terms is surpassed by the introduction of increasingly suggestive coined terms and metaphorical uses. Already begun by Husserl and Heidegger, Merleau-Ponty accepts and expands the vocabulary of newly coined terms, *life-world, being-in-the-world, intersubjectivity, lived body,* and to these adds a series of at least seemingly metaphorical uses of *silence, incarnation, gestural meaning, singing the world.*

The coined terms are quasi-technical from the beginning, despite their odd ring to the uninitiated. *Lived body (corps vécu)*, for example, is meant both to contrast with the objectified sense of body used in the sciences and to refer to a primary, nonreduced sense of living being as embodied being. Similarly, *intersubjectivity* is meant to contrast with the Cartesian state of private selves and to positively suggest that we are already "outside ourselves in the world."

Even as technical terms much of their strength comes from evocations not found in the traditional and key terms of (a). This evocative sense is stronger yet in the metaphorical uses. The silence which precedes and which indirectly conveys meaning within speech, "singing the world" which precedes the philosophical norm of conceptualized meaning, pushes us further toward a radical and different philosophical vocabulary.

    c) Although there is a continuum of radicality from metaphor to the importation of words from spheres not previously used by philosophers, to my mind the most radical and interesting use of language comes into greater prominence with Merleau-Ponty's later writing. *The Visible and the Invisible,* itself an evocative and suggestive title, brings us *flesh, chiasm, intertwining, perceptual faith,* and *wild Being.* This is "wild language" more akin to a literary genre than to much philosophy. Merleau-Ponty's struggle with language leads him beyond the strategy of transforming terms to the initiation of a radical discourse.

What we are seeing here can be stated quite simply, although the reality which is embodied in this development of language is far from simple. Simply, as the implications of the phenomenological revolution become more clear the more radical the use of language becomes. The new wine threatens to burst the older philosophical wineskin. We are witnessing a birth of philosophical meaning. This is the case even if we must allow that the rent of the wineskin may eventuate in the dissolution of philosophy as it was previously known; that, at least, is one possibility. The emphasis within Merleau-Ponty's theory of language upon the genesis of meaning is thus both a result of the demands of the phenomenological turn *and* a reflection upon Merleau-Ponty's own philosophical experience.

The anti-Cartesian polemic of the *Phenomenology of Perception* forms the background against which both the emergent theories of perception and expression take shape. The argument which rejects both empiricist and intellectualist interpretations of perception and speech is one which attacks any notion of dualistic "purity." Both traditional interpretations maintain a *pure* (psychological) mental being and a *pure* (mechanical) material being. In contrast, the existential theory, based upon a phenomenological interrogation of experience, claims that such purity is constructed, not found.

Rejected are all notions of pure data, sensory or conceptual. Accepted is an essential ambiguity of the perceptual object, an incompleteness, an openness to multiple possibilities, all of which Merleau-Ponty argues is true to the actual perceptual experience. Rejected are both the objective (mechanical) body and a transparent intelligence (mind) as immediate interpretations of experience. Accepted is the embodied subject whose every action is subject to an initial movement from the unformed to the formed, whose gesture precedes any later attained clarity of intellection. Rejected is an objectively given world whose reality is merely to be discovered (constructed) by the right method of formal geometricization. Accepted is a world which is always pregnant with significance, but whose meaning must be rewon through an interrogation of its presence. The life-world appears between the subject and the world within the focus of perception.

The outcome of this line of thought on a functional level is to recognize that any theory of the body is already a theory of perception and, inversely, that any theory of perception is already a theory of the body. Thus the complete overthrow of both versions of Cartesianism, empiricism, and intellectualism is implied. The outcome on the ontological level is the rejection of the psychophysical dualism which pervades the sciences of man, and the affirmation of an existential ontology of embodiment as the root source from which any adequate theory of body and perception must arise.

The lived body, the embodied subject immersed in a world pregnant with unwon significance becomes the basic theme of the existential version of the primary perceptual situation. This unitary and relational ontology is held to transcend the dualism of Cartesianism.

The theory of expression in the *Phenomenology of Perception* is situated within and patterned after and upon the theory of perception. It follows the same polemic pattern vis-à-vis the Cartesianism of dominant linguistic theory that the theory of perception follows in relation to psychophysical dualism. This is the Cartesianism which makes language psychophysical. "Physical" *sounds,* in the case of speech, are the pure body-matter of language, while "psychological" *meanings* are the mind of language. These two separate and distinct realms of linguistic being are related in some way in actual language.

While it is important to see how the Cartesianism of the linguistic sciences is isomorphic with that of other forms of psychophysical dualism, it is more important here to begin to discern the existentialist alternative concerning language posed by Merleau-Ponty. This alternative again parallels what was done with the theory of the body and perception. Language, expression, is ontologically always found *embodied.* "The word has a meaning." [4] Merleau-Ponty's whole theory of language is one of embodiment.

The argument is essentially the same as that used for the lived body: the concrete experience of speech and language is always first and primordially one of embodied meaning. A pure sound without significance is a construct; phonemes, morphemes, etc., are conceptual "explanations" of sounds—they do not occur within concrete experience. But so is a pure thought! Both are the linguistic equivalents of sense data, the objective body, and the mental activity of the empiricist and intellectualist traditions. They are constructions which "explain" the ambiguities of experience. Linguistic "mechanics" on one side and pure "intelligence" which merely uses language as a tool on the other both fall short of noting the concrete incarnation of meaning which Merleau-Ponty offers as the existential alternative.

"The word has a meaning" is the linguistic equivalent to the embodied subject. "The meaning of words must finally be induced by the words themselves . . . immanent in speech." [5] Existent language is embodied expression, while both a presignificant sound and a postlinguistic thought are dualistic constructions. Embodied, expressive meaning thus parallels the embodied, perceiving subject.

This theory of embodied meaning is, I believe, the central focus around which the usually noted features of Merleau-Ponty's language theory radiates. Both (1) the "return to the speaking subject" and (2) the "primacy of speech" usually remarked upon by commentators are dependent in their significance upon the central notion of embodied meaning.

Furthermore, what must be seen as inextricably tied to the key of embodied meaning is the method of phenomenological genesis which Merleau-Ponty sees as his nuanced divergence from Husserl. The phenomenology of genesis is what creates the full *existentiality* of this phenomenology. Not only does it seek to "put essences back into existence," [6] to think back to the life-world, but the weight given to genesis ultimately overcomes the sense of essence entirely. That "the greatest lesson which the reduction teaches us is the impossibility of a complete reduction" [7] is not so much a negative comment upon Husserl as it is the affirmation of what Merleau-Ponty understands an *existential* phenomenology to be.

This use of a phenomenologically described genesis *is* both what uncovers and justifies the sense of embodied meaning Merleau-

Ponty elaborates. Symptomatically it is instructive to note the main class of examples which he uses to illustrate the phenomenon of expressive embodiment. The paradigms come from learning new meanings: 1) the child learning speech, 2) on first understanding others, 3) learning a new language, 4) learning a new philosophy, 5) the lover revealing his feelings, 6) the writer or philosopher struggling with awakening a sense of primordial experience, and finally 7) the mythical "first man who spoke." [8] These examples, adumbrated in varying ways, once again are illustrations of the stylistic movement of Merleau-Ponty's thought: the movement from an initial ambiguity through struggle toward a birth of new meaning. Thus for a third time we are plunged into the thematic problem of speaking in such a way that the new may be expressed. How does one give birth to the position which is phenomenology?

If a theory of embodied meaning is central—"the word has a meaning"—there remains a need to outline the configuration of that embodiment. Merleau-Ponty notes "there is thus, either in the man who listens or reads, or in the one who speaks or writes, a *thought in speech* the existence of which is unsuspected by intellectualism." [9] Thought-in-speech, to coin a language version of being-in-the-world, is the expressive dimension of human existence. What is embodied expression?

1) First, it is clearly a behavior or performance of the living subject. Language, in Merleau-Ponty's sense, is not something *had* by a subject, it is the subject in action. Speech in the broad sense used by Merleau-Ponty is the *performance* of thought. "Thus speech, in the speaker, does not translate ready-made thought, but accomplishes it." [10] The same performative emphasis is found in the interpretation of naming, that speech-act so often taken as central to linguistically oriented philosophies: "The denomination of objects does not follow upon recognition; it is itself recognition" [11] and "For the child a thing is not known until it is named, the name is the essence of the thing and resides in it on the same footing as its colour and its form. For pre-scientific thinking, naming an object is causing it to exist or changing it . . ." [12] Naming *is* a performance.

2) The expressive activity of the subject in speech is intentional, directed, and focused activity. And as with all phenomenological

intentionality, such an action is both internal and external, or better, already outside the enclosed self and directed toward the world. The performance of thought internally is as linguistic as actually spoken thought. "Thought is not 'internal' then, and does not exist independently of the world and of words . . . we can silently recall to ourselves, . . . through which we acquire the illusion of an inner life. But in reality this supposed silence is alive with words, this inner life is an inner language." [13] "Inner speech" is also embodied expression. Language is not private—nor is it public—it is between subjects, intersubjective, it is "a synchronizing of my own existence, a transformation of my being. We live in a world where speech is an *institution*." [14]

3) One can better say, rather than that man has or uses language, that man *is* language. "Language is much more like a sort of being than a means . . ." [15] The thought-in-speech is a style of living in language: "The linguistic and intersubjective world no longer surprises us, we no longer distinguish it from the world itself, and it is within a world already spoken and speaking that we think." [16] This thought-in-speech in which we live is itself quite concrete and even particular: "We may speak several languages, but one of them always remains the one in which we live. In order completely to assimilate a language, it would be necessary to make the world it expresses one's own . . ." [17] Embodied expression is concrete and positional, the place from which one views the world. There is no metalanguage of disembodied meanings floating over and apart from actual languages: "If there is such a thing as universal thought, it is achieved by taking up the effort towards expression and communication in *one* single language, and accepting all its ambiguities, all the suggestions and overtones of meaning of which a linguistic tradition is made up, and which are the exact measure of its power of expression." [18] Thought-in-speech is embodied language. Thought *is* body in the same way that the subject is body.

If linguistic dualism is rejected, there is no realm of ideal and complete meanings above and apart from actual language, nor is there a realm of pure physical nonmeaningful motion which may be "used" by mentally employed meanings. And if all language in the human sense is existentially embodied, then the result is that the performances, positionings, and utterances we make are all made "inside" this existential language. Our being is being-*in*-the-world, here our thought is *in* language. But this poses an enigma: "One would have to know the language in order to learn it." [19]

Merleau-Ponty accepts this enigma: "This sort of circle, according to which language, in the presence of those who are learning it, precedes itself, teaches itself, and suggests its own deciphering, is perhaps the marvel which defines language." [20] Language does convey itself. Although there are several neat conceptual devices developed by Merleau-Ponty to justify this totality of engagement within language—for example, the first word of a child functions as a sentence, the part is already a whole [21]—it is more important to grasp the internal movement which characterizes the birth of speech.

This movement, again the birth of meaning, is one which follows the pattern *from ambiguity toward clarity*. In Merleau-Ponty's phraseology this is the movement *from silence to speech*. Several important aspects of this movement need to be noted:

4) Strictly speaking there is no state of meaning prior to existential language. We have been led astray by those who have spoken of a "prelinguistic" state insofar as we have been led to believe that this state is equivalent to a state prior to meaning. There is, in Merleau-Ponty, the movement from silence to speech, but that is not a movement from nonmeaning to meaning; it is rather a movement from the implicit to the explicit, from ambiguity already *pregnant* with significance to the expressed significance of speech. If meaning is "born" it is because the world is already pregnant with that possibility.

Meaning, in an existential theory of language, is the entire movement from silence to speech. It is a ratio of the implicit to the explicit. Thought, in the usual sense, is but a focus within the totality of meaning. "Because meaning is the total movement of speech, our thought crawls along in language. Yet for the same reason, our thought moves through language as a gesture goes beyond the individual points of its passage." [22]

5) It is within the context of this movement from implicit to explicit significance that the continuum of metaphors and behaviors which surround explicit speech takes shape. "Gesture," "gestural

meaning," even the "indirect voices of silence" in painting, and the concrete meanings of music which so well illustrate the incarnation of sound and meaning are all in between silence and speech. They are meaning-activities of the subject, but short of the explicitness of speech.

6) If the first movement is from implicit to explicit, from silence to speech, a reverse side of that movement remains implied in every speech-act. There is no final, no complete expression. "Now if we rid our minds of the idea that our language is the translation or cipher of an original text, we shall see that the idea of complete expression is nonsensical . . ." [23] The existentiality of language is such that the field of implicit silence is always broader than the focus of explicit speech. In this sense speech is essentially finite even if also open and indeterminate.

7) It also means that the broad field of silent, implicit meaning lies as present background to all that is actually said. "Behind" what is said lies the unsaid. For Merleau-Ponty this is to imply that all speech, all explicit language, is *indirect*: "But what if language expresses as much by what is between words as by words themselves? By that which it does not 'say' as by what it 'says'? . . . All language is indirect or allusive—that is, if you wish, silence." [24]

The existentiality of Merleau-Ponty's language theory begins in anti-Cartesianism. In this it is part of the entire movement of phenomenology to counter the dualistic division of man and his world into matter and mind and instead to reassert the essential insertion of man within his world as incarnate being in a life-world. The existentiality of Merleau-Ponty's theory of language ends in the affirmation of embodied expression, thought-in-speech, and speech-in-silence, which attempts for language what is also attempted for the subject in the world.

All the various parts and aspects of Merleau-Ponty's theory of language may be seen as a Gestalt, a coherent whole, when viewed as the exemplification of a basic phenomenological model. For the sake of simplicity I shall use the terms *field* and *focus*. The field is the totality of presence which may be differentiated according to the question addressed to this totality of presence. Thus, if our question is visual, the field is the whole of the visual field before one. Focus is the region within the field which is attended to. Again, if the example is visual, the focal center may be a certain object which stands out against the background of the visual field. (I have characterized both here in noematic terms, but the noetic reflexiveness might also be characterized. For example, that which stands out must be correlated to my act of attending.) Extended, the notion of field, is the phenomenological world; focus, the phenomenologically explicit attention within the world.

Silence, in Merleau-Ponty's use, is the field of pregnant, latent expressiveness always already present to the living subject. Pregnant silence is always and wholly present; man lives within the world of implicitly meaningful silence. "In short, we must consider speech before it is spoken, the background of silence which does not cease to surround it and without which it would say nothing." [25] *Speech* is the focal center, the explicit foreground of meaning which floats, varies, is directed but which always stands out against the background of silence. The clarity of explicit meaning is a relative clarity, relative to the implicitness of the background. ". . . The clearness of language stands out from an obscure background, and if we carry our research far enough we shall eventually find that language is equally uncommunicative of anything other than itself, that its meaning is inseparable from it." [26] The movement of speech is a movement from and upon the field of silence.

This is also the reason why speech is the taking of a position. Focusing is taking a position within the field; it is a selection. But it, too, is relative. The position does not remove or obliterate the field, it merely allows it to remain background. The "indirection" of silence behind speech is not removable, and equally the explicitness of focus is not capable of completeness. If speech is necessarily focus it can easily be seen that completeness of expression is impossible. Completeness belongs latently only to silence, to the unsaid.

The focus against the field may be exceedingly fine or broadened. Thus within speech itself—better speech within language—the focus is the moving ray situated within the world of silent meaning. "Since the sign has meaning only insofar as it is profiled against other signs, its meaning is entirely involved in language. Speech always comes into play against a background of speech; it is always only a fold in the immense fabric of language." [27]

From the primordial field of silence to the most explicit attainment of thought-in-speech also lies a concentric and leveled set of stratifications. Gestural meaning, if "lower" than speech, is also broader. Within speech itself such stratifications also occur: "any linguistic operation presupposes the apprehension of a significance, but that significance in both cases is, as it were, specialized: there are different layers of significance, from the visual to the conceptual by way of the verbal concept." [28] But these stratifications are merely fine distinctions within the broader concept of field and focus which are called for to differentiate the degree and range of the focal center.

All expressivity, whether "higher" or "lower," more or less finely focused, is a positioning within the world of pregnant silence. Concretely, in man's case, thought-word-sound in existential speech is the region where expressivity is most clearly heard. The posturing which is speech *is* singing the world and "singing the world" is now stronger than metaphor.

One may even speak here of expressivity as an "essence" of man in spite of Merleau-Ponty's demur concerning essences. Expressivity is at the least a dimension of being-in-the-world which takes distinctive human shape in speech. But it may be more than *a* dimension.

In Merleau-Ponty's works the question of language was imbedded in and followed from his discoveries within the perceptual world. Expressivity in the *Phenomenology of Perception* was but one chapter, even at that titled "the *body* as expression, and speech [emphasis mine]." The other explicit essays, paragraphs, comments, also constitute but a small amount of the whole. Yet there is reason to believe that the reversed role of language in relation to perception taken here shows something at work in Merleau-Ponty's thought as well.

If expression is always embodied and if the world itself is that field of pregnant silence, then language in its broadened sense is not just one dimension of being. My thesis is that the result of taking language in the way Merleau-Ponty has *is to have made the question of perception enigmatic.* Furthermore, I believe that Merleau-Ponty in the later works had himself begun to reevaluate the role of perception. Perception, in *The Visible and the Invisible,* becomes the "perceptual faith." But faith recognized as faith is already doubt. "Philosophy is the perceptual faith questioning itself about itself. One can say of it, as of every faith, that it is a faith *because* it is the possibility of doubt . . ." [29]

This doubt is such that perception and language are tied together more intimately, more inextricably than ever. If perception is "primary," it is not bare perception. Although Merleau-Ponty maintains his notion of inquiring back and down into the levels of experience—to the degree that he leaves himself open to those who see him seeking a level of prelinguistic meaning—that which is found is always sayable. Philosophy "asks of our experience of the world what the world is before it is a thing one speaks of and which is taken for granted, before it has been reduced to a set of manageable, disposable significations; it directs this question to our mute life, it addresses itself to that compound of the world and of ourselves that precedes reflection . . ." [30] But what it finds there is already open to speech. "But in addition, what it finds in thus returning to the sources, *it says.*" [31]

What is at issue can be put quite simply if viewed tangentially in terms of another broadly accepted philosophical distinction. Phenomenology in its anti-Cartesianism claims to have rediscovered the living subject in a life-world. This rediscovery claims the power to overthrow the Cartesian notions of psychophysical dualism; mind and matter are to be transcended. However, a similar and no less tenacious distinction haunts our intellectual world as well, the distinction between *nature* and *culture*. Broader in its way, and thus perhaps more difficult to dispel, this dichotomy must fall, too, if phenomenology is to work out its program. Given this distinction, perception in its way belongs roughly to nature, while language belongs more clearly to culture. Thus language is "added" to nature.

There is evidence in Merleau-Ponty of an ambivalence with respect to the tradition of nature versus culture. In his essay, "The Primacy of Perception," he appears to overtly appeal to the distinction; [32] in the *Phenomenology of Perception* he speaks of speech as "the surplus of our existence over natural being" [33] and links language to "a linguistic world and a cultural world," [34] but increasingly the implication is one which must eventually call the nature-culture dualism into question. From the beginning he admits that human perception is different from animal perception, though without linking this to culture as such. But in *The Visible and the Invisible* perception becomes enigmatic precisely in relation to "cultural" factors. For example, in noting dramatic changes in the history of art regarding perspective, "I say that the Renaissance perspective is a cultural fact, that perception is polymorphic and that if it becomes Euclidian, this is because it allows itself to be oriented by the system." [35] Perception here is strongly relative to culture. But inversely, Merleau-Ponty notes, "What I maintain is that: there is an informing of perception by culture which enables us to say *that culture is perceived.*" [36]

Nowhere, to my knowledge, does Merleau-Ponty make a sustained attack upon nature-culture dualism as upon the previous distinction of psychophysical dualism, but the ambiguity of perception, now tied more thoroughly to that of meaning, language, and culture calls for that attack to be made. But how? The answer is found in the guiding theme of the need for a radical language in phenomenology. If we are to "see" in a new way we must be able to "say" in a new way. A language needs to be born.

Man as language has this capacity. His perceptual meanings (the *life-world* in the best Husserlian sense) are open to the creation of the new. Merleau-Ponty was on this track when he was untimely taken:

If this paradox is not an impossibility, and if philosophy can speak, it is because language is not only the depository of fixed and acquired significations, because its cumulative power itself results from a power of anticipation or of prepossession, because one speaks not only of what one knows, so as to set out a display of it—but also of what one does not know, in order to know it—and because language in forming itself expresses, at least laterally, an ontogenesis of which it is a part.[37]

Phenomenology as philosophical revolution in its "linguistic tactics" is implicitly and purposefully radical in direction. It is precisely that which is taken for granted which must be uprooted and, if need be, overthrown. Cartesian clarity is sometimes at opposite poles with the *poesis* necessary for radicalness. "But from this it follows that the words most charged with philosophy are not necessarily those that contain what they say, but rather those that most energetically open upon Being, because they more closely convey the life of the whole and make our habitual evidences vibrate until they disjoin." [38] What Merleau-Ponty begins to seek explicitly lay earlier in latent form in both the phenomenological turn and in the question of embodied, expressive being. What must be said may be said, but not in terms of what merely has been said. What is called for, given the logic of Merleau-Ponty's thought, is "wild meaning." [39]

3
Alphonso Lingis

BEING IN THE INTERROGATIVE MOOD

THE DIFFERENT chapters of the fragmentary text of *The Visible and the Invisible* we have are structured into a polemic against empiricist operational thought, reflective analysis, negativist, dialectical, and intuitionist modes of thought; the work sets out to define an essentially, intrinsically interrogative mode of cognition—a "question-knowing." [1] And throughout, *The Visible and the Invisible* sustains a polemic against every kind of positivism—the positivism of empiricism, but also that of reflective philosophy (with "all the positivist bric-a-brac of 'concepts,' 'judgments,' 'relations' . . ." [2]), the positivism of Being in itself which is, in Sartre, the counterpart of the negativist conception of mind proper to dialectical thought, the positive essences presupposed by phenomenological intuitionism, and the positive intuition of immediate existence in Bergsonism. The ontology it was preparing proposes that Being itself is not to be positively conceived, that "the existing world exists in the interrogative mood," [3] "in a sort of gliding, beneath the yes and the no." [4] What could it mean to conceive Being itself in the interrogative mood? What could be the purpose of such a project?

The first chapter of *The Visible and the Invisible* recalls the last chapter of Hume's *Inquiry concerning Human Understanding*. It concerns the origin of that vacillation in our relationship with Being which is doubt. Perception is contact with Being; it is indeed the primordial contact. This contact elicits a kind of adherence, to which Hume already ascribed the psychological-religious term *faith.* Seeing is believing. To see is to see the things themselves; the world is what we see.[5]

But this faith is unstable. It is even intrinsically destined to break up; perception itself contests itself. Every appearance of being gives itself out as provisional, as subject to further confirmation; the definitive contact with Being itself is "always further on." [6] "Everything that *is* could *not be,*" said Hume, but that was for him a speculative fact; it meant that the concept of the inexistence of any being never involves logical incompatibility. Merleau-Ponty finds contingency in the immediate data, in the very intuitive appearance of existent beings; "each perception envelops the possibility of its own replacement by another, and thus of a sort of disavowal from the things." [7] The break-up of the perceptual appearances, their crossing one another out, their canceling of one another [8] continually disrupts the adhesion to the perceived elicited in the perceptual contact; the primordial contact we have with Being is labile.

Doubt originates then in perception and because of the nature of the contact with being effected in perception. The inconsistencies, discordancies within the flux of sensible appearances prevent us from blindly trusting our senses alone, Hume says; we have to correct their evidences by reason.[9] The instability of perceptual appearances provokes us to seek fixed criteria of truth and error which have to be forged by the intellectual operations of reason; with the aid of rational criteria we seek to build up a system of propositions representing the universe of objects existing in themselves.

Yet, for Hume, this labor only issues in a new doubt—speculative doubt or posterior skepticism. Reason posits a domain of objects existing in themselves, to which our sole access is our uncertain perception. We can discount those factors in our perceptual experience which vary as our organs vary, we can strip the appearances of the secondary qualities, but that does not authorize us to posit the residue as representing the objects themselves as they are in themselves. For we find that representations of the primary qualities of the objects take form with and through the secondary qualities, which we know to represent the way we are affected rather than the way the objects themselves are. And we are witnesses only of the representations that form and dissipate about us; we do not and can not witness the process by which they take form, by which they are allegedly caused in us by objects existing in themselves.[10] Belief in this causation sustains the rational labor to form discriminations within the dubious perception, but "the least philosophy" exposes the dubious moorings of this rational faith. "The 'natural' man," as Merleau-Ponty puts it, "holds on to both ends of the chain, thinks *at the same time* that his perception enters into the things and that it is formed this side of his body. Yet coexist as the two convictions do without difficulty in the exercise of life, once reduced to theses and to propositions they destroy one another and leave us in confusion." [11]

Hume finds again, then, in the order of propositions the same skepticism inevitable in the perceptual life; the order and coherence of our propositions turns out to be not more solid than the order and cohesion of the things with which contact is made in perception. And yet the generalized skepticism does not succeed in instigating in Hume a reflection on the nature of the being with which we have such dubious contact; thought, subjecting itself to critical self-examination and training itself in the mood of skepticism, continues to posit a world of objects existing in themselves, against which to exasperate its suspicion of itself. The moments of doubt occurring in the perceptual life—the "skepticism prior to study and philosophy"—concern the subsistence of the objects that appear; the Humean cultivated skepticism, posterior to science and research, is an incrimination of the "imperfection of our organs."

The Humean skepticism is hence an epistemological skepticism that tacitly contains an ontological dogmatism. Extreme attention to the manner of proceeding cognitively is accompanied by an eclipse of attention to the manner of being of what emerges primordially. The spontaneous belief in beings whose existence appears as the reason for and *telos* of the perceptual experience reappears, in the order of critical cognition, in the form of the protoscientific belief in pure objectivity, such that the reflexive and critical operation of cognition, "far from dissipating the obscurities of our naïve faith in the world, is on the contrary its most dogmatic expression, presupposes it, maintains itself only by virtue of that faith." [12] All the critical suspicion of modern philosophy is directed to the manner of proceeding of the imperfect subject— "as if one already knew what to exist is and as if the whole question were to apply this concept appropriately." [13]

"For us the essential is to know precisely what the being of the world means." [14] The type of philosophy Merleau-Ponty wishes to found is one for which the doubt inherent in perceptual life provokes not a reflective thought—a return of the subject suspiciously, critically, upon itself—but an inquiry into the meaning of the being with which contact is made in the uncertain perception. Merleau-Ponty is not simply searching for a new epistemological *method*.

The forms of thought successively examined in *The Visible and the Invisible*—the self-sufficient operational thought of positivist science, the reflective thought of criticist epistemology, the negativist thought of dialectical philosophy, the intuitionist thought assembling moments of insight into essences (phenomenology) or into concrete existents (Bergsonism) —are so many methods of overcoming the dubious perceptual experience, of making contact with an objectivity or with a subjectivity, existing in themselves. They represent not so much different inquiries into the meaning of the world's Being as methods more critical than perception to make contact with a Being whose format has been presupposed. Merleau-Ponty's book undertakes first a systematic program of casting into question the ontological presupposition of these forms of thought.[15]

But the form of thought *The Visible and the Invisible* intends to introduce is not entitled "interrogative thought" simply because it elaborates a polemic against other forms of thought which tacitly presuppose what the vacillations of perceptual faith should lead us to question—the meaning of the primary emergent being. It is a form of thought that discovers that *the existing world itself exists in the interrogative mood.*[16] This means that the distances and the vacillations and the negativity that make contingency be contingency and possibility be only possibility are in being itself and are not simply shimmerings of nothingness playing over the positivity of being due to the imperfection of our organs or due to the void in the core of subjectivity through which being is seen.[17] The discordance and contestation by which beings crowd out one another, eclipse one another, and push one another into depth and into latency are not just contingencies of the way beings are seen by our imperfect organs or by our insubstantial subjectivity nihilating itself continually; they are what makes beings be and be there.

The form of thought, then, that would discover and pursue the meaning, the plot, of Being itself would itself have an interrogative form—but not because doubt would have forced it to recognize that it is out of contact with Being; it would not be a provisional state of expectation, provoked by doubt or by speculative skepticism, destined to be concluded and eliminated by positive cognition, by the epiphany of a plenary Being that resolves all interrogation. Here interrogation would itself be a form of knowing, a form of contact with being—and the maximal degree of contact.

The effective, present, ultimate and primary being, the thing itself, are in principle apprehended in transparency through their perspectives, offer themselves therefore only to someone who wishes not to have them but to see them, not to hold them as with forceps or to immobilize them as under the objective of a microscope, but to let them be and to witness their continued being—to someone who therefore limits himself to giving them the hollow, the free space they ask for in return, the resonance they require, who follows their own movement, who is therefore not a nothingness the full being would come to stop up, but a question consonant with the porous being which it questions and from which it obtains not an answer, but a confirmation of its astonishment.[18]

Thus while classical epistemology grounds its universalized doubt or its skepticism in the natural doubt inevitable in the course of experience that makes contact with being, Merleau-Ponty seeks to build an interrogative form of thought that would express and exhibit the interrogative scheme of the primary world horizon.

Modern epistemology saw in perception a natural alternation of faith and doubt. Hume said that by "natural instinct" we believe in the existence of what appears in perceptual experience; by natural instinct, and prior to all philosophy, all reflection, we believe in the real and doubt illusions. And in *Phenomenology of Perception*

Merleau-Ponty accepted the Husserlian terms *Urdoxa* and *Urglaube*: the perceptual experience is an apparition of sensible forms which elicit and motivate a "faith" or "primordial opinion." [19] To speak of "faith" means, he notes later, in *The Visible and the Invisible,* "an adherence that knows itself to be beyond proofs, not necessary, interwoven with incredulity, at each instant menaced by non-faith." [20]

Yet, in a note added to the first page of *The Visible and the Invisible,* Merleau-Ponty already expressed a scruple: "the notion of faith has to be specified." There is in fact already something wrong in seeing in perception an alternation of acts of faith and of doubt. Faith and doubt are already reflective acts, and in specifying the modalities of perceptual experience with these terms, Hume and Husserl already introduce intellectual operations into perception. [21] This is visible in Hume, for whom the faith antecedent to philosophy is of the same order as the speculative or rational faith consequent upon critical examination, as the doubt from which philosophy arises—the antecedent skepticism—is of the same order as the doubt into which philosophy issues—the posterior skepticism. But, on the one hand, "perception is not a science of the world, it is not even an act, a deliberate taking up of a position." [22] And perception is not contact with the true or the credible, but with the real—which is not exactly the same thing.

To believe is to believe as true; to perceive is to perceive the real. It is true that moments of contact with reality, like moments of insight into the truth, are interconnected; the real forms a continuous fabric, as the true forms a coherent system. But the solidity and cohesion of the real is not that of the manifest connections by which the true is grounded upon antecedents. [23] "My field of perception is constantly filled with a play of colors, noises and fleeting tactile sensations which I cannot relate precisely to the context of my clearly preceived world, yet which I nevertheless immediately 'place' in the world, without ever confusing them with my daydreams. Equally constantly I weave dreams round things. I imagine people and things whose presence is not incompatible with the context, yet who are not in fact involved in it: they are ahead of reality, in the realm of the imaginary." [24]

Thus the perceived is not the grounded; it is not that which is manifestly consistent with its context of explicit connections and supported by its antecedents. It is not the true. It is not the certain; it is not that which provokes in the subject the essentially reflexive experience of certainty.

But the perceived is not then to be characterized as possible or probable. The perceived makes its appearance as a configuration of the world which awaits its confirmation from the subsequent flux of world apparition, and which contains in germ in itself a sort of intuitive potentiality for its own replacement by another configuration which would "cross it out" or "cancel" it. Afterward, retroactively, "we seek in vain in this chalky rock what a moment ago *was* a piece of wood polished by the sea." [25] The index of reality that is invested in the new appearance is lifted from the prior one. This means, then, that this appearance and the one that will replace and cancel it do not have the status of successive possibilities, or hypotheses successively entertained, and that the appearance that was destined to be canceled did not have the status of the "merely conceived," of simply subjective origin. It radiated forth from the world itself, as did the appearance that canceled it, and each gives itself out not as probable but as real.

The perceptual field then does not consist in moments of credibility, probability and improbability, and consequently the "notion of faith [has] to be specified. It is not faith in the sense of decision . . ." [26] It is not an act or an initiative; it is not preceded by a survey of the antecedents and the context; it is not a commitment to one hypothesis rather than to another.

And, correlatively, when firm contact with the world begins to dissolve, and gives way to the buzzing of phantasms, [27] when the movement of existence into the world reverses into a retreat into the margin of the world inhabited by the ghosts of things, [28] this is not acts of doubt replacing the natural instinct of faith. The monocular images which represent phantasms are not repudiated by an act of doubt in the passage to the binocular vision that reaches the real; they mature into it, and are absorbed by it like residues of it or sketches of it. [29] What effects this passage is not an act of doubt provoking critical reexamination; it is the body which concentrates and centers itself.

Instead, then, of specifying, rendering precise the notion of faith, *The Visible and the Invisible* will abandon it in favor of the concept of an original interrogative relationship with Being.[30] "It is necessary to comprehend perception as this interrogative thought that lets the perceived world be rather than posits it, before which the things form and undo themselves in a sort of gliding, beneath the yes and the no." [31] Interrogation is "the ultimate relation to Being and . . . an ontological organ." [32] Our primary contact with being is then not belief in the manifest, the true, but "a continual enterprise of taking our bearings on the constellations of the world." [33] What is deficient in credibility is itself something of being; we are offered not being itself, definitively, but rays, radiations of being, dimensions of exploration.

But to determine perceptual experience as inaugural interrogation rather than faith and doubt requires now that the notion of interrogation be specified. This vital interrogation is not simply the alternation of faith and doubt, of position and negation, of affirmation and denial, of expectation and satisfaction, of demand and response. Merleau-Ponty *opposes* it to dialectics. ". . . The interrogative is not a mode derived by inversion or by reversal of the indicative and the positive, is neither an affirmation nor a negation veiled or expected, but an original manner of aiming at something, as it were a *question-knowing,* which by principle no statement or 'answer' can go beyond and which perhaps therefore is the proper mode of our relationship with Being, as though it were the mute or reticent interlocutor of our questions." [34] This interrogation is not a state of ignorance, void, nothingness, destined to be filled by the epiphany of the positive; it is the form of relationship with a world that forms and remains a horizon,[35] a field of contingencies, potentialities, perspectival deformations, "which thus is staggered out in depth, conceals itself at the same time that it discloses itself, is abyss and not plenitude." [36] Questioning then must be understood as the active manner of keeping in contact with a being that is and remains at a distance, contracts and dilates its presence, contests and negates its own course.

Questioning then is not a state of noncontact, a negativity, due either to the absence of being or to the subject first mired in its own nothingness—the phenomenology of questioning does not lead to an ontology of the subject as nothingness. Questioning is, to be sure, a state of "gaping openness" [37] about which a horizon of things recedes into distance and into indifferentiation. But this does not happen because, by moments, contact with being is lost (moments of doubt, of subjectivity cocooned in mirages created by its own spontaneity) ; it occurs because "he who sees is of [the world] and is in it." [38] "No question goes toward Being: if only by virtue of its being as a question, it has already frequented Being, it is returning to it." [39]

It is the implantation of the seer in the world that makes the world appear to him as a horizon—that is, a field-structure where every surface prolongs itself into depth, where every configuration prolongs itself, in the expanse of time and space, into a dimension. It is the very force and evidence of this implantation here—a fact of concentration of existence, of ecstatic, diasporic existence having a site—that makes the distances, the distension, and the progressive indifferentiation of being manifest as such.[40]

This implantation is not immanence or mutual inscription. Idealism sees in the inaugural perception a consciousness constitutive of things; realism sees in it a consciousness simply receptive of the things. Both conceive of the things as objects posited in perception, and both conceive of the perceptual relationship, when effective, to be one of adequation between subject term and object term. To conceive of the perceptual relationship as interrogative is to completely reject the concept of adequation at the basis of both idealism and realism; [41] it is also consequently to conceive in an essentially new way the nature of the perceived field. To perceive is not to posit a term with which, then, the subject would be, due to its having constituted it or due to its having passively received it, in a relationship of adequation; perception is rather essentially differentiation, gradation, specification of distances, formation of tensions, reliefs, contrasts.[42] To not perceive something is not for a positive content to cease to be there before the subject; it is for there to be disarticulation, undifferentiation, for there to no longer be contrast, divergency, relief.[43] What we perceive then is not a positive term existing in itself and supporting its own "properties"; what we perceive is a contrast, a tension—not an adequation with our substance, but a difference from us, marked out in the continuous fabric of being, of "flesh," of which we too are a part. It is that divergency, that contrast, that is the perceptual meaning, the sense grasped in perception;[44] meaning has not a positive but a differential being.[45] For Merleau-Ponty the term *interrogation* was intended to name perception as an operation of making differences and distances appear. ". . . We have with our body, our senses, our look, . . . *measurants (mesurants)* for Being, dimensions to which we can refer it, but not a relation of adequation or of immanence. The perception of the world and of history is the practice of this measure, the reading off of their divergence or of their difference with respect to our norms."[46]

If perceptual experience is finite and ever nondefinitive, provisional, interrogative, then, if the world appears in the format of a horizon, a field of continually receding differentiation, this is not to be ascribed simply to the "imperfection and inexactitude of our organs." To do so is to maintain the regulative ideal of a fully positive and fully determinate epiphany of being in itself—a phantasm the Pyrrhonian paradoxes show us we must definitively reject.[47] It is true that our organs are imperfect and inexact, but being cannot exhibit itself and spread itself out without receding into horizons of indifferentiation.[48] How and why this is so is the central question of an interrogative ontology. We can note that Heidegger's whole work since *Being and Time* has been preoccupied by the effort to say what is this one movement by which Being is simultaneously epiphany and occultation, by which Being shows itself and hides itself. *The Visible and the Invisible* sets out to determine this movement in quite new terms.

What is at stake in the longest chapter of *The Visible and the Invisible,* that entitled "Interrogation and Dialectic" (at first sight a more developed version of Merleau-Ponty's political polemic with Sartre first argued out in print in *Les aventures de la dialectique*) ,[49] is the repudiation of the speculative concepts of position and negation, being and nothingness, for an interrogative ontology. Nothingness can only posit the positive being in itself; it cannot differentiate, grade, organize in depth and in degrees into plurality of planes.[50] The differentiation and occultation of being then is not a negative event; being is not so much hidden as harbored—delayed, postponed—by itself. What follows is that we have to abandon the idea of being conceived in the affirmative mode, the image of being that is projected as the self-subsistent correlate of our positive, lucidly grounded judications.

In *Being and Nothingness* Sartre had argued that what supports, what makes possible, the presence, that is, the being-there-before-us of the sensible phenomena is a certain form of being—is self-identity, is being posited in itself. And existentialist philosophy was built on the interpretation of the essence of subjectivity as a movement of transcendence; subjectivity is existence for itself because it is first existence transcending itself; for this reason also it is contact with being outside of itself.

For Merleau-Ponty of *The Visible and the Invisible*, transcendence is the inner plot, the ontological format, of the things themselves. What is transcendence? It is existing not in self-identity but in autodispersion; it is being beyond oneself, outside of oneself, ecstatically; it is existing in multiple location; it is existing not as a point-occupancy in space and in time, but as a radiation, a dimension, as a "world-ray"; it is not to be in-itself, but "always further on." [51] The dramatic transfer of the concept of transcendence from the analysis of the inner nature of subjectivity to that of the type of being constitutive of phenomena "requires a complete reconstruction of philosophy." [52] This development in *The Visible and the Invisible* situates the late ontology of Merleau-Ponty at the extreme antipodes of the philosophy of *Being and Nothingness*.

The Visible and the Invisible finds transcendence in its scrutiny of the mode of being of sensible phenomena.[53] The sense-datum is not a quale, "a pellicle of being . . . at the same time indecipherable and evident"; [54] it is rather a "certain differentiation, an ephemeral modulation of this world," [55] a "punctuation in a field," [56] that is, a hiatus, a caesura, a contrast, a "certain node in the weave of the simultaneous and the successive," [57] a "quality pregnant with a texture, the surface of a depth, a cross-section upon a massive being, a grain or corpuscle borne by a wave of Being." [58] This is to say that the sense-datum does not exist in self-identity; it has the form of a dimension and not a point, a differential pattern across time and space rather than the factitial occupancy of a spot of time and space; it is utterly referential. It makes an appearance at a location only by forming, crystallizing, or precipitating a medium.[59] And this is precisely what gives it its opaque, sensorial *presence*; "what is indefineable in the *quale,* in the color, is nothing else than a brief, peremptory manner of giving in one sole something, in one sole tone of being, visions past, visions to come, by whole clusters." [60] Thus "the sensible is precisely that medium in which there can be *being* without it having to be posited; the sensible appearance of the sensible, the silent persuasion of the sensible is Being's unique way of manifesting itself without becoming positivity." [61]

Thus there is a reticence built into the way beings become present to us, "as though [Being] were the mute or reticent interlocutor of our questions." [62] With this form of being there can be no adequation—only interrogation.

To be sure, there is a transcendency in the sensorial subject too; sensibility is movement from oneself to the being that presents itself. But this transcendence is not the ground of the presence of phenomena; it is itself elicited, sustained, and continually provoked anew by the very transcendence of the things. It is in this way that perception has the form of a questioning, a quest after things that are there from the start—from the beginning there is contact; they are where they are, but are also radially where we are, *because* transcendence is their being—but from the start recede in spatio-temporal trajectories, eliciting our movement after them.

The ontological discourse that expresses, that thematizes, the topology of a world existing in the interrogative mood shall itself have an essentially interrogative form. That does not imply that it be a discourse in the grammatical form of interrogative sentences, or that it be a systematic inability to make affirmations. It shall be a thought that says what it says not in formulas, where unknown terms are determined by relationship with known terms, and ideally in algorithm, but in an operative language which would express in its lateral movements, its metaphors, its transversal organization, the identifiable style, the structural laws, the regular relationships and the latent logic [63] of the things themselves. A true "coincidence, a

manner of making the things themselves speak" "would be a lan-
guge of which [the philosopher] would not be the organizer, words
he would not assemble, that would combine through him by virtue
of a natural intertwining of their meaning, through the occult trad-
ing of the metaphor—where what counts is no longer the manifest
meaning of each word and of each image, but the lateral relations,
the kinships that are implicated in their shiftings and their exchanges." [64] It is assuredly a vast problem to set up such a form of
discourse, and find for it criteria by which we can be sure it truly is
"bringing the things themselves, from the depths of their silence,
to expression." [65] Merleau-Ponty undertook this work in the fragmentary manuscript *La prose du monde*,[66] by way of an extensive
investigation into the origin of expressive forms.

This kind of interrogative ontology shall not be a foundational
enquiry in the classical sense. Classical epistemology based itself on
the doubt perception itself inevitably contains; by rendering that
doubt reflective and systematic, extending it into a methodic doubt
or a generalized skepticism, epistemology subjects the moments of
dator perception to cross-examination, so as to provide for cognition truly credible primary data. It thus functions as a foundation
for science—not to guarantee the methodological exactitude of
scientific observation of phenomena, but to guarantee their status
ontologically—their status as beings that can be credibly posited as
existing in themselves. In doing so it contributed to building up a
cognition that means to posit in the absolute our naïve faith in a
world existing in itself.

The ontology Merleau-Ponty intended to build was not meant
to secure data that would exhibit being in itself, to certify the naïve
belief in the world in itself that positivist science takes up on its
own account without dissipating its obscurities.[67] And yet contemporary science itself—in its operations on astronomical spaces and
microphysical realities, as well as in its developments in the psychology of perception and social psychology—has learned to situate
physically the physicist and to situate sociohistorically the psy-
chologist. In these developments, which Merleau-Ponty followed
throughout his career, he saw an implicit abandon of the positivist
conception of objective being which classical epistemology was

intended to sanction. In restoring to view the total fabric of the brute world, from which our ideas of subjects and of objects have been lifted by abstraction,[68] the interrogative ontology will be able to show the origins of the "strangest" ideas of contemporary science [69] in our perceptual contact with being. Then in its own way the interrogative ontology will function to illuminate the bases of science.

4

Raymond Herbenick

MERLEAU-PONTY AND THE PRIMACY
OF REFLECTION

READERS of and commentators on Merleau-Ponty's early philosophical work tend to assign a primacy to perception. Usually, the primacy accorded to visual, auditory, tactile, spatial, temporal, gestural, and erotic forms of perception is characterized as ontological. Here *ontological* may mean: 1) that prereflective levels of experience are the basis upon which reflective experience occurs; 2) that prereflective experience is the origin from which reflective experience emerges; 3) that the concept of prereflective experience is much broader than that of reflective experience; or 4) that the concept of prereflective experience has a priority over that of reflective experience. Each of these possible interpretations of the thesis of the primacy of perceptions seems consistent with Merleau-Ponty's own remarks delivered in 1946 after the publication of the *Phenomenology of Perception* before the Société française de philosophie and later published under the title, "The Primary of Perception and Its Philosophical Consequences." In that address Merleau-Ponty considered an objection to his thesis of the primacy of perception, namely, that to go back to the unreflected is to renounce reflection.[1] Rather, "it is the unreflected which is understood and conquered by reflection."[2] Thus, Merleau-Ponty argues, reflection should not be carried away with itself or feign ignorance of its origins in perceptual experience. But it can and should be used to render prereflective experience intelligible.

So long as the primacy of perception is regarded as an ontological claim about the character of human experience, few conceptual difficulties arise. But if the claim is construed as other than an ontological claim, a number of problems may appear. For example, if the primacy of perception is interpreted as an epistomological or methodological claim, it follows that reflective discourse about human experience is rejected or at least disallowed since Merleau-Ponty would be claiming that perception is to be known only by perception.[3] And if it is logically odd to assert that perception is to be known only by perception, there seems to be no way in which Merleau-Ponty can offer a description or explanation of human experience.

But such an interpretation is unwarranted, for it presumes that from a methodological standpoint Merleau-Ponty rules out in principle or in practice a reflective method for the study of the various forms of perceptual activities and dispositions. However, rather than reject reflective procedures, Merleau-Ponty in his early works seems to have held to the primacy of reflection so far as epistomological or methodological claims are concerned.

In order to show the plausibility of the primacy of reflection in the early major philosophical works of Merleau-Ponty, the following points will be considered: 1) the disposition toward phenomenological positivism; 2) the purported objectives of phenomenological positivism; 3) the use of the two chief methods of phenomenological positivism; and 4) the results obtained by the use of the methods of phenomenological positivism. Afterward, a brief examination of the doctrine of the later writings will be attempted.

It is understandable that no reference would normally be made to Merleau-Ponty's work in a history of positivist thought such as Kolakowski's recent work, *The Alienation of Reason: A History of Positivist Thought,* although sporadic and surprisingly sympathetic references to Husserl are frequent.[4] Yet such an omission is unfortunate inasmuch as Merleau-Ponty's outlook in his early works is a self-confessed positivism. Certainly he saw little affinity between his work and that of the members of the Vienna Circle [5]—although it might be argued that his concern with the *Lebenswelt* (life-world) and the later Wittgenstein's interest in *Lebensformen* (forms of

life) bear great resemblance. Yet, following Husserl, he credited
Hume as having gone "in intention, further than anyone in radical
reflection, since he genuinely tried to take us back to those phenomena of which we have experience, on the hither side of any formation of ideas,—even though he went on to dissect and emasculate
this experience." [6] And in the preface to the *Phenomenology of
Perception* he accoladed the eidetic method of phenomenology as a
"method of phenomenological positivism" which bases the possible
on the real.[7]

In subscribing to phenomenological positivism, certain commit-
ments are requisite in Merleau-Ponty's view. First, there must be the
recognition of an underlying indeterminancy in human experience,
a positive phenomenon having no place in either empiristic or in-
tellectualistic positions.[8] Such recognition supposes that the phenomenal field of experience or the context of human experience
"places a fundamental difficulty in the way of any attempt to make
experience directly and totally explicit." [9] That is not to say that the
phenomenal field is unknowable nor to say that methods for knowing the phenomenal field cannot be successful. But it does suggest
certain limits to knowledge and to ourselves as knowers, namely,
that the phenomenal field of experience is sampled by man according to conceptual models however distinct or explicit.[10] This leads
to the second requirement which might be called the "fallibility of
conceptual models of human experience." According to Merleau-
Ponty, one should avoid the mistake of reifying conceptual models
despite the tendency to reify: "The physicist's atoms will always
appear more real than the historical and qualitative face of the
world, the physico-chemical processes more real than the organic
forms, the psychological atoms of empiricism more real than perceived phenomena, the intellectual atoms represented by the 'significations' of the Vienna Circle more real than consciousness, as long
as the attempt is made to build up the shape of the world (life, perception, mind) instead of recognizing, as the source which stares us
in the face and as the ultimate court of appeal in our knowledge of
these things, our *experience* of them." [11]

That last requirement of phenomenological positivism is of prime
importance to scientific endeavors which make use of conceptual

models. In particular, Merleau-Ponty has in mind the use and abuse of conceptual models or schemes in anatomical, neurological, and psychoanalytic studies. In the former, the phenomenal field of experience can be conceptually modelled along the lines of the stimulus-response structure of reflex arc theory, while in the latter, it can be conceptually modelled along the lines of the stimulus-response structure found in the theory of the unconscious. Conceptual models in both contexts serve to describe and explain the phenomenal field of experience for experimental purposes. So long as they do not become "misleading analogies" in Wittgenstein's sense or become "myths to hide behind" in Merleau-Ponty's sense, these conceptual models are entirely appropriate for experimental objectives, although one must recognize the possibility that empirical events may require revisions in these conceptual models or complete change from one conceptual model to another. Merleau-Ponty's criticism of the reification of the stimulus-response schema in reflex arc theory and in the theory of the unconscious further illustrates this antireductionistic requirement of phenomenological positivism:

Synaesthetic perception is the rule and we are unaware of it only because scientific knowledge shifts the centre of gravity of experience, so that we have unlearn how to see, hear, and generally speaking, feel, in order to deduce, from our bodily organization and the world as the physicist conceives it, what we are to see, hear, and feel.[12]

It would be a mistake to imagine that even with Freud psychoanalysis rules out the description of psychological motives, and is opposed to the phenomenological method: psychoanalysis has, on the contrary, albeit unwittingly, helped to develop it by declaring, as Freud puts it, that every human action "has a meaning," and by making every effort to understand the event, short of relating it to mechanical circumstances.[13]

Lastly, there is the recognition of the complementary character of perspectival and conceptual models. By this Merleau-Ponty means that phenomenological positivism, like anthropology, should "neither try to prove the primitive is wrong nor to side with him against us, but to set itself up on a ground where we shall both be intelligible without any reduction or rash transposition." [14]

The early writings of Merleau-Ponty can be looked upon as examples of phenomenological positivism. Typically, *The Structure of Behavior* is regarded as a critique of classical reflex arc descriptions and explanations of human behavior; while the *Phenomenology of Perception* is taken as a proposal of "intentional arc" descriptions of human action. But such characterizations tend to overlook the methodological primacy of reflection common to both works. In order to elucidate this thesis of the primacy of reflection it will be helpful to note the doctrine common to both works and examine the apparent objectives of phenomenological positivism.

The central doctrine of *The Structure of Behavior* and the *Phenomenology of Perception* is that of human action. In the former, Merleau-Ponty remarks that the objective of the work is to link consciousness with action in order to enlarge the idea of human action.[15] In the latter, he calls for a view of the phenomenal body as the center of potential action over a milieu.[16] And he does so by virtue of the fact that the main areas of the phenomenal body are devoted to action such that my body can be said to be wherever there is something to be done.[17] Phenomenological positivism's chief concern is thus appropriately to describe and properly understand *human* action. Such tasks undoubtedly require some type of reflective methodology, the outlines of which are apparent in numerous statements of specific objectives by Merleau-Ponty.

In *The Structure of Behavior* Merleau-Ponty argues that the scientific study of human action does not require the omission of certain "aims of life" or purposes often noticed in such human activities as daily conversations, productive work, or dressing oneself with clothes and various ornaments.[18] That is to say, one can appropriately use expressions emblematic of means and goals to describe certain human activities. Nor need there be an omission of the concepts of intention, utility, or subjective value in order to understand certain human actions.[19] At the same time, it may be possible and desirable for experimental purposes to reduce apparent intentional behavior to an anatomically based conceptual model of regulated, preestablished nerve pathways and circuits.[20] But this does not *ipso facto* preclude other possible conceptual models for explaining human actions, either for experimental purposes or nonexperimental purposes. Likewise, the reduction of the human body to a mosaic of sensations and of human perception to pure sensations need not exclude other explanatory moves, even that of other reductions.[21] Finally, the projection of elementary reactions artificially isolated from a natural context to more complex responses embedded in a natural context does not preclude erroneous extrapolations and therefore other explanations.[22]

From the preceding, it is clear that Merleau-Ponty does not discount scientific reflection pursued for purposes of experimental description and explanation. Rather, he seems to be arguing that experimentally designed descriptions and explanations of human action do not methodologically require the elimination of intentional phenomena, and further that elementary anatomical-neurological models should be reckoned as dispensable conceptual models. His point is that the successful use of certain conceptual models of human actions tends to produce exaggerated claims about human action. For example, an irreconcilable opposition might be maintained between blind autonomic systems and intentional activities, or certain escape-mechanisms might be used as significant explanatory principles.[23] Such claims and escapisms no doubt run counter to phenomenological positivism. But Merleau-Ponty also views them, much as did C. S. Pierce, as obstacles to scientific inquiry.

In the *Phenomenology of Perception* Merleau-Ponty argues the inadequacy of certain philosophical appraisals of human action as found in the empiricist and intellectualist traditions. The "pure sensation," the "association of sensations," and the "projection of memories," conceptual models of human perception adhered to by classical empiricism, rely upon "blind processes" in which there is *"nobody who sees."*[24] Intellectualist models based on attention or judgment convert the perceiving subject into an "acosmic" subject and thus tend to either fall short of or overshoot the human perceptual life that is to be understood.[25] In short, the empiricist "cannot see that we need to know what we are looking for, otherwise we would not be looking for it," while the intellectualist fails to realize that "we need to be ignorant of what we are looking for, or again there would be no need for looking."[26] Both positions run counter to phenomenological positivism since they use inadequate conceptual models, reify their models, and fail to recognize indeterminacy.[27] But Merleau-Ponty is quick to point out that neither totally overlooks the natural world.[28] In fact, he notes that both can build up equivalents of the sundry structures of experience and thus construct "some semblance of subjectivity." [29] Still the better alternative is to use the conceptual model furnished by phenomenological positivism as in the case of models based on attention. Merleau-Ponty thus writes: "Now attention has to be conceived on the model of these originating acts, since secondary attention, which would be limited to recalling knowledge already gained, would once more identify it with acquisition. To pay attention is not merely further to elucidate pre-existing data, it is to bring about a new articulation of them by taking them as *figures*." [30] In this passage Merleau-Ponty unequivocally asserts the need for an appropriate conceptual modelling of a feature of human experience.

From the above, it is evident that Merleau-Ponty does not reject philosophical reflection pursued for purposes of understanding.[31] The decision-problem is not the possibility or impossibility of reflection, but that of the adequacy of certain conceptual models of human activities proposed in empiricist and intellectualist philosophical circles. The suggested criterion of inadequacy for "testing" such conceptual constructions as the "reflex arc," the "unconscious," "pure sensation," the "association of sensations," the "projection of memories," "attention" and "judgment" is that of pointing out everything that is made incomprehensible by their use.[32] And it is one which, in accord with phenomenological positivism, Merleau-Ponty will apply to his conceptual construct of the "intentional arc" which serves as an alternative description of human action.

Granted Merleau-Ponty's interest in both pointing out the inadequacies of certain conceptual models of human action and proposing an alternative conceptual model, a question arises concerning the further specification of the criterion of inadequacy. Simply stated, the rule prescribes that a conceptual model is adequate so long as its use does not make what is modelled incomprehensible, and otherwise inadequate. Although Merleau-Ponty in the early works does not consider explicitly and systematically the meaning of *incomprehensible,* it can be inferred that in *The Structure of Behavior* the whole perceptual context should be made comprehensible by conceptual models of human experience.[33] In the *Phenomenology of Perception* it is "integrated experience" that should be made comprehensible through conceptual models of human action.[34] Whatever the terminology, it is clear that Merleau-Ponty counts a conceptual model as adequate if it recognizes that reflective experience is dependent upon prereflective experience and to the degree that it emphasizes this dependency.[35] Thus, a conceptual model of human action may fail to be adequate in two ways at least: 1) that it fails to explicitly recognize the dependency of the reflective on the prereflective; and 2) that it explicitly recognizes that dependency but fails to recognize the degree of dependency in its formulation.

To recognize the dependency and the degree of dependency of the reflective upon the prereflective, Merleau-Ponty indicates the availability of at least two methods of radical reflection. The first method is through "living the body" and the second one is through adopting "a new way of looking at things." The former acknowledges that the experience of one's own body runs counter to a reflective method that distinguishes the phenomenal field into subject and object, while the latter reverses the relative positions of the clear and the obscure in such a way that it can abundantly elucidate phenomena and thus be said to be justified according to the criterion of inadequacy.[36] Before untangling Merleau-Ponty's use of and reflection upon these two methods of radical reflection for phenomenological positivism, it will be helpful to consider J. L. Austin's distinction between "demonstrating the semantics of a word" and "explaining the syntactics of a word."

In his article, "The Meaning of a Word," Austin suggests that in ordinary life situations at least two types of responses are possible to a question of the sort: "What is the meaning of the word *racy*?" [37] The first response possible is what Austin calls "explaining the syntactics of the word *racy* in the English language." Here one can try to reply in words by describing what raciness is and what it is not, or, by giving examples of sentences in which one might use the word and others in which one does not or should not use the word. For example, one might utter the sentences, "That novel was racy" and "That race riot was racy" in order to show possible uses and misuses of the word *racy* in a natural language common to the inquirer and the respondent. The second possible response, however, is non-linguistic in character and involves what Austin calls "demonstrating the semantics of the word *racy*." Here one tries to get the questioner to imagine or even to actually experience situations which the respondent could describe correctly by means of sentences containing the words, *racy, raciness*, etc., and again other situations which he could describe incorrectly by means of sentences containing the word and its cognates. For example, one might thrust a vial of ammonia near the nose of the inquirer to allow him to experience an instance of raciness or use appropriate hand gestures to indicate that a particular novel is a literary masterpiece. According to Austin these two procedures could be used in the case of most ordinary words to come to an understanding of the use of a word as well as to test someone at length on his understanding of the word. However, Austin acknowledges that in coming to understand a word and in testing for the understanding of the word in question, the two procedures "perhaps could not be entirely divorced from each other." [38]

Austin's distinction between "demonstrating the semantics of a word" and "explaining the syntactics of a word" for ordinary life situations is extremely suggestive for understanding Merleau-Ponty's distinction between the two forms of radical reflection. For Merleau-Ponty, "living the body" mentioned in the early works serves to impart a certain experience rather than function as a new principle or new way of rendering human action intelligible. It is the second method of radical reflection—later called intentional analysis and existential analysis—that serves to impart a new way or new principle for rendering human experience intelligible.[39] Thus, as a form of reflection, "living the body" may be viewed as analogous to "demonstrating the semantics of a word" inasmuch as both are used to promote understanding. This is especially evidenced by Merleau-Ponty's attempts to lead his readers to an understanding of pre-personal experience.[40] However, there is one important dissimilarity, namely, that Austin's "demonstrating the semantics of a word" is nonlinguistic in character whereas for Merleau-Ponty "living the body" appears to be linguistic in character and thus more akin to "explaining the syntactics of a word." This difficulty in interpretation, however, may be obviated if one takes seriously the point made by Austin that the two procedures may not be entirely divorced from each other. And one could also argue that Merleau-Ponty merely mentions these ways of "living the body" and reports linguistically on the nonlinguistic uses of them to impart experiences. If so, two forms of reflection may still be distinguishable.

As a form of reflection, "intentional analysis" may also be taken as an analogue to "explaining the syntactics of a word." The similarity lies in the resort to language for purposes of conceptual analysis insofar as both procedures attempt to state or exemplify what counts and what does not count as falling under some concept. This too is evidenced by Merleau-Ponty's analysis of the concepts of personal and prepersonal experience. One important dissimilarity must be noted, however. Austin's syntactical explanation is used to indicate the linguistic meaning of a word within a relatively stable natural language. But Merleau-Ponty's intentional analysis is to be used to introduce a new set of linguistic terms and to develop a new conceptual framework or technical language. In *The Structure of Behavior* he remarks that "it is not a question of risking one hypothesis among others, but of introducing a new category, the category of 'form', . . . whose existence in experience is confirmed without a vitalist hypothesis." [41] And in the *Phenomenology of Perception* he states:

It is precisely Gestalt psychology which has brought home to us the tensions which run like lines of force across the visual field and the system constituted by my own body and the world, and which breathe into it a secret and magic life by exerting here and there forces of distortion, contraction and expansion. The disparity between retinal images, and the number of intermediate objects do not act either as mere objective causes producing from outside my perception of distance, or as demonstrative reasons for it. They are tacitly known to perception in an obscure form, and they validate it by a wordless logic. But what Gestalt psychology lacks for the adequate expression of these perceptual relationships is a set of new categories: it has admitted the principle, and applied it to a few individual cases, but without realizing that a complete reform of understanding is called for if we are to translate phenomena accurately.[42]

Now that a contrast has been developed between the procedures noted by Merleau-Ponty and Austin, further characterizations and illustrations of the two forms of radical reflection can be given.

Throughout his early philosophical works, Merleau-Ponty makes mention of the method based upon "living the body" and often comments on what can be accomplished through its use. For example, one should be able to: 1) return to the world of actual experience prior to the objective world; 2) reawaken one's experience of one's body and one's world; 3) revive perceptual experience buried under its own results; 4) resume contact with sensory life lived within; and 5) reachieve a direct and primitive contact with the world as one lives it.[43] Such procedures thus serve to impart experiences for reflective consideration rather than to engage in a reflective analysis according to some conceptual construct. This does not imply that the experiences imparted cannot be reflected upon, for it is possible to use a "hybrid procedure" of finding an example among these imparted experiences, stripping it of its facticity, and elucidating it by varying it through the imagination and then thinking upon the invariable element of mental experience.[44] It is in this sense that "living the body" can be said to yield descriptions without the construction of conceptual models of a higher order, although there is no reason to suppose that these descriptions cannot be used to exemplify conceptual constructs. The following citations can be viewed as illustrative of Merleau-Ponty's understanding of what "living the body" means in his two early major philosophical works:

I know very well that I will never see my eyes directly and that, even in a mirror, I cannot grasp their movement and their living expression. For me, my retina is an absolute unknowable. This is, after all only a particular case of the perspectival character of perception.[45]

At the very moment when I live in the world, when I am given over to my plans, my occupations, my friends, my memories, I can close my eyes, lie down, listen to the blood pulsating in my ears, lose myself in some pleasure or pain, and shut myself up in this anonymous life which subtends my personal one.[46]

The fact that my earliest years lie behind me like an unknown land is not attributable to any chance lapse of memory, or any failure to think back adequately: there is nothing to be known in these unexplored lands. For example, in pre-natal existence, nothing was perceived and therefore there is nothing to recall.[47]

In the first quotation above from *The Structure of Behavior* it is clear that the attempt to perceive one's eyes directly or indirectly can lead one to recognize the perspectival character of perceptual experience or possibly prereflective experience. In the last two quotations from the *Phenomenology of Perception* it is evident that the attempt to listen to one's blood pulsating in one's ears or to remember something about one's prenatal experience can lead one to recognize the anonymous character of prereflective experience. All three citations thus show how "living the body," although merely mentioned by Merleau-Ponty, can be used to impart certain experiences for reflective consideration.

Merleau-Ponty also mentions "intentional analysis" in both of his early works. Through this form of radical reflection which broadens the notion of intentionality to include both the intentionality of acts and operative intentionality, one should be able to go back to the experience to which words such as *feeling, seeing,* and *hearing* refer and thus redefine them along intentional lines.[48] More precisely, intentional analysis is to: 1) make man's effective involvement in the world amenable to conceptualization; 2) make explicit the prescientific life of consciousness; and 3) circumscribe the phenomenal field.[49] To accomplish this Merleau-Ponty specifies several descriptive guidelines. The tasks are:

. . . trying to describe the *phenomenon* of the world, that is, its birth for us in that field into which each perception sets us back, where we are as yet still alone, where other people will appear only at a later stage, in which knowledge and particularly science have not so far ironed out and levelled down the individual perspective.[50]

. . . to give a direct description of our experience as it is, without taking account of its psychological origin and the causal explanation which the scientist, the historian or the sociologist may be able to provide.[51]

The guidelines for understanding are:

. . . take in the total intention—not only what these things are for representation (the "properties" of the thing perceived, the mass of "historical facts," the "ideas" introduced by the doctrine) — but the unique mode of existing expressed in the properties of the pebble, the glass or the piece of wax, in all events of a revolution, in all the thoughts of a philosopher.[52]

. . . seek an understanding from all these angles simultaneously. . . . All these views are true provided that they are not isolated, that we delve deeply into history and reach the unique core of existential meaning which emerges in each perspective.[53]

Technically, parts 1 and 2 of the *Phenomenology of Perception* are reserved for these tasks of intentional analysis. However, in part 3 Merleau-Ponty attempts a "phenomenology of phenomenology," that is, to explain human action in terms of temporal intentionality after noting the inadequacy of intentional analysis for explanatory purposes.[54] Although remarks by Merleau-Ponty on methodological guidelines are few, it is clear that intentional analysis does have some explanatory force. For example, after describing the operative forms of intentionality shown by the phenomenal body in motor, sensory, expressive, erotic, perceptual, spatial, and temporal activities, Merleau-Ponty postulates an "intentional arc" upon which these processes are based. Borrowing the term from Fischer's *RaumZeitstruktur und Denkstörung in der Schizophrenie,* Merleau-Ponty claims that it: 1) goes limp in a patient whose experience has disintegrated; 2) endows experience with its degrees of vitality and fruitfulness in the normal person; 3) subtends one's conscious cognitions, desires, and perceptions; 4) projects one's past, future, and physical, ideological, and moral situation comprising the human setting; 5) brings about the unity of the senses and intelligence, of sensibility and motility, etc.; 6) conditions the unity and disunity of experience; and 7) comes to dwell in a molecular edifice.[55] This undoubtedly is intended by Merleau-Ponty to have great explanatory force. But it should be noted that this intentional arc or *UmWelt-Intentionalität* is characterized by Merleau-Ponty as a single intention inferred from the phenomena of the body's synergy and therefore has the status of an inferred entity.[56] Intentional analysis therefore can be said to have some explanatory potential just as it can be said to describe human experience. "Experience of phenomena," Merleau-Ponty states, "is not, then, like Bergsonian intuition, that of a reality of which we are ignorant and leading to which there is no methodical bridge—it is the making explicit or bringing to light of the prescientific life of consciousness which alone endows scientific operations with meaning and to which these latter always refer back. It is not an irrational conversion, but an intentional analysis." [57]

To illustrate Merleau-Ponty's use of intentional analysis the following quotations may be cited:

Certain states of adult consciousness permit us to comprehend this distinction. For the player in action the football field is not an "object," that is, the ideal term which can give rise to an indefinite multiplicity of perspectival views and remain equivalent under its apparent transformation. It is pervaded with lines for force (the "yard lines"; those which demarcate the "penalty area") and articulated in sectors (for example, the "openings" between the adversaries) which call for a certain mode of action and which initiate and guide the action as if the player were unaware of it. The field itself is not given to him, but present as the immanent term of his practical intentions; the player becomes one with it and feels the direction of the "goal," the horizontal planes of his own body. [58]

. . . "living" (*leben*) is a primary process from which, as a starting point, it becomes possible to "live" (*erleben*) this or that world, and we must eat and breathe before perceiving and awakening to relational living, belonging to colours and lights through sight, to sounds through hearing, to the body of another through sexuality, before arriving at the life of human relations. [59]

The first citation above from *The Structure of Behavior* shows the results of applying the method of intentional analysis to an example of lived-experience. Here Merleau-Ponty recognizes the distinction between the lived and the known and attempts a description of the participants's experience in a football game. In the second quotation from the *Phenomenology of Perception,* it is clear that Merleau-Ponty is also using the method of intentional analysis in indicating the relationship between the anonymous processes of life and personal relationships. In both cases he relies upon the concept of *Fundierung*, the founding-founded relationship, which is a noncausal relation of "originator to originated" introduced explicitly in part 3 of the *Phenomenology of Perception*: ". . . the founding term, as originator—time, the unreflective, the fact, language, perception—is primary in the sense that the originated is presented as a determinate or explicit form of the originator, which prevents the latter from reabsorbing the former, and yet the originator is not primary in the empiricist sense and the originated is not simply derived, since it is through the originated that the originator is made manifest." [60]

Apparently this founding-founded relation serves as the conceptual model of human experience and thereby as the presupposition of intentional analysis. Other passages tend to support this interpretation as well. However, not all of them are readily identifiable as products of "living the body" or of "intentional analysis" as in the following case: "But what, in the sleeper and the patient, makes possible a return to the real world, are still only impersonal functions, sense organs, and language. We remain free in relation to sleep and sickness to the exact extent to which we remain always involved in the waking and healthy state. . . ." [61] Here Merleau-Ponty may have been referring to the results of the use of both types of procedures which may indicate that the two forms of radical reflection are not divorced from each other. No doubt this may spawn difficulties for readers of Merleau-Ponty's early works. But it should not lead one to overlook the methodological primacy of reflection in Merleau-Ponty's phenomenological positivism, especially the primacy of intentional analysis.

By using the two procedures of radical reflection, Merleau-Ponty has moved in a direction similar to that of P. F. Strawson. Briefly, Strawson argues that certain facts about one's body (for example, eyeball orientation) explain why a person feels peculiarly attached to his body, regards his body more favorably than any other, and why he speaks of his body as his. But these facts do not explain why one should have a concept of one's self as a person nor why corporeal characteristics should be ascribed to him as a person. Such an explanation requires that the term *person* be taken as logically prior to such derivative expressions as *animated body* and *embodied anima*. [62]

No doubt Merleau-Ponty's objective is comparable to Strawson's, namely, to indicate a logically primitive term that can be used to identify human behavioral particulars and that is free from dualism. But his category preference differs considerably from Strawson's since it is guided by the method of intentional analysis along with its presuppositions of the founding-founded relation. For Merleau-Ponty the expression, *"être-au-monde,"* functions as a fundamental category.[63] Used to designate the intentional structure of a particular human behavioral whole, the expression may yield derivative terms such as *subject, world, customary body, momentary body, natural world, cultural-human world, prepersonal experience,* and *personal experience* through intentional analysis. It should be noted that intentional analysis thus allows material predicates (for example, white, tall), personal predicates (for example, joy, belief), cultural predicates (for example, usury, incest) and prepersonal predicates (for example, tonus, sleep) to be ascribed to whatever falls under the category of *être-au-monde.* In short, it purports to show a way in which one can speak of human action as fundamentally intentional. It regards the assumption that all human action is nonintentional as erroneous and the assumption that all human action is nonintentional as fraught with *ad hoc* criteria. Instead it assumes quite simply that all human action is intentional in degrees.

It may be that Merleau-Ponty's early philosophical program runs aground on its resort to a priori genetic psychology, as Strawson might charge. It may also encounter serious difficulties in trying to show that all conceptual models, whether experimentally based or philosophically based, are complementary. But in light of these discussions of Merleau-Ponty's phenomenological positivism and of the methods of radical reflection one cannot fault this program on the grounds that it can provide no reflective methodology for discoursing about human action. Instead, one must address oneself to this methodological thesis of the primacy of reflection.

At first glance, it appears that Merleau-Ponty rescinds the methodological primacy of reflection through "living the body" and "intentional analysis." For example, in *The Visible and the Invisible* several precautions about philosophical reflection are raised. These are as follows: 1) a philosopher's manner of questioning is not that based on cognitions;[64] 2) philosophy aims at a universe which does not in principle admit of objectifying procedures or reflective approximation; [65] 3) the methods of proof and of cognition invented by thought already established in the world, the concepts of *object* and *subject* it introduces, do not enable us to understand what the perceptual faith is; [66] 4) if philosophy declares itself to be reflection, it prejudges what it will find; [67] 5) each time we want to get at perceptual faith, or lay hands on it, or circumscribe it, or see it unveiled, we do in fact feel that the attempt is misconceived, that it retreats in the measure that we approach it; [68] 6) we do not allow ourselves to introduce into our description concepts issuing from reflection, whether psychological or transcendental.[69]

Such precautions, however, are directed primarily at certain types of philosophical positions and methodologies rather than at reflection per se. In view of the advances in contemporary physics and psychology, the resort to Cartesian analysis through the concepts of subject and object should be contested by physicists and psychologists as well as by philosophers.[70] The objective and subjective sides of experience are to be construed as "two orders hastily constructed within a total experience, whose context must be restored in all clarity." [71] Since science presupposes this fundamental relationship of perceptual faith and does not elucidate it, it is the task of philosophy to somehow elucidate it.[72] And this elucidation consists in a reflection that philosophy must perform.[73]

Now at least three philosophies are faulted by Merleau-Ponty for rendering impossible an understanding of perceptual faith or *ouverture-au-monde*.[74] These are the philosophies of reflection, dialectics, and intuition. The philosophy of reflection is a conversion to reflection that omits the genesis of the world and of the idealizations of thought from its concerns. It evokes and requires as its foundation a "hyperreflection." [75] The philosophy of dialectics attempts to restore one's contact with the unreflected but in so doing compromises "our power of reflection." [76] At best it only prepares the way for a suitable understanding of perceptual faith. The philosophy of intuition in searching for essences or in calling for fusion with things amounts to a positivism that philosophical reflection rejects.[77]

Now in criticizing these types of philosophical method Merleau-Ponty often laments the "positivism of language" to which they succumb since the questions raised by each are not "radical enough." [78]

Yet, it is "by considering language that we would best see how we are to and how we are not to return to the things themselves." [79] Merleau-Ponty also remarks:

The words most charged with philosophy are not necessarily those that contain what they say, but rather those that most energetically open upon Being, because they more closely convey the life of the whole and make our habitual evidences vibrate until they disjoin. Hence it is a question whether philosophy as reconquest of brute or wild being can be accomplished by the resources of the eloquent language, or whether it would not be necessary for philosophy to use language in a way that takes from it its power of immediate or direct significance in order to equal it with what it wishes all the same to say.[80]

It is this move by Merleau-Ponty to use language in the philosophical interrogation of perceptual faith to "catch sight of this strange domain" that augurs the methodological primacy of reflection.[81]

Perhaps the best direct statements of the methodological primacy of reflection appear in chapter I of *The Visible and the Invisible,* entitled "Reflection and Interrogation." Objecting to the philosophy of reflection for ignoring "the origination and the derived," Merleau-Ponty points out that his remarks concerning reflection were "nowise intended to disqualify it for the profit of the unreflected or the immediate (which we know only through reflection)." [82] And he states: "It is a question not of putting the perceptual faith in place of reflection, but on the contrary of taking into account the total situation, which involves reference from the one to the other. What is given is not a massive and opaque world, or a universe of adequate thought; it is a reflection which turns back over the density of the world in order to clarify it, but which, coming second, reflects back to it only its own light." [83] Thus, the moment that the reflective effort tries to capture that relationship called "openness upon the world *(ouverture au monde)* " one will miss it and then be able to catch sight of the reasons that prevent it from succeeding and of "the way through which we would reach it." [84] The reflective operation that could reach this fundamental relationship is what Merleau-Ponty terms "hyperreflection." More fundamental than the conversion to reflection, hyperreflection is to "take itself and the changes it introduces into the spectacle into account." [85]

Such reflection proceeds then in the wake of interrogations, rather than through the prior specification of what one could find or should find.[86] Yet this hyperreflection guarantees nothing. "We know," Merleau-Ponty says, "neither what exactly is this order and this concordance of the world to which we thus entrust ourselves, nor therefore what the enterprise will result in, nor even if it is really possible." [87] Interrogation gives access to the too little noticed "cross regions of experience" but without knowing in advance "what our interrogation itself and our method will be." [88] As he also says in the working notes, "but in reality all the particular analyses concerning nature, life, the human body, language will make us progressively enter into the *Lebenswelt* and the 'wild' being, and as I go along I should not hold myself back from entering into their positive description, nor even into the analysis of the diverse temporalities." [89] It is clear from the preceding that Merleau-Ponty still holds to the primacy of reflection. But does this mean that he still retains the use of the methods, "living the body" and "intentional analysis"?

In *The Visible and the Invisible* Merleau-Ponty still mentions various ways of "living the body." These may be seen in his comments on binocular perception, on seeing red things, and on seeing one's own retina.[90] Through these techniques of consulting, making explicit, frequenting, and comprehending the world from within, an appropriate elucidation is possible.[91] This is especially evident in Merleau-Ponty's comments on the phenomenon of reversibility of the seeing and the visible, the touching and the touched.[92] There Merleau-Ponty seems to report on the results of a demonstration of the semantics of the term, *reversibility*—something open to his reader's field of experience or imagination.

While the preceding instances clearly indicate Merleau-Ponty's resort to "living the body," there are others that exhibit "intentional analysis." For example, in criticizing the philosophies of reflection of Spinoza and Kant, Merleau-Ponty argues that both ignore "the origination and the derived" or the founding-founded relation articulated in his early works.[93] And in his working notes on the rationalism-irrationalism dilemma he points out that to dissolve the dilemma one must recognize that "a consciousness is intentionality without acts, *fungierende*" and that "the chiasm, the intentional 'encroachment' are irreducible." [94] Besides these scant references to intentional analysis in the criticism of certain philosophies, there are others that show Merleau-Ponty's use of this method of analysis in presenting the first results of his interrogations.

Noting that the basic concept involved is that of the "flesh," Merleau-Ponty alludes to "clear zones" and "opaque zones" in attempting to describe this fundamental relationship of "openness upon the world" or "perceptual faith" which takes place by "a sort of chiasm." [95] He states,

I experience—and as often as I wish—the transition and the metamorphosis of the one experience into the other, and it is only as though the hinge between them, solid, unshakeable, remained irremediably hidden from me. But this hiatus between my right hand touched and my right hand touching, between my voice heard and my voice uttered, between one moment of my tactile life and the following one, is not an ontological void, a non-being: it is spanned by the total being of my body, and by that of the world; it is the zero of pressure between two solids that makes them adhere to one another. My flesh and that of the world therefore involve clear zones, clearings, about which pivot their opaque zones, and the primary visibility, that of the *quale* and of the things, does not come without a second visibility, that of the lines of force and dimensions, the massive flesh without a rarefied flesh, the momentary body without a glorified body.[96]

This move is reminiscent of Merleau-Ponty's attempts in the early works to elucidate "integrated experience," the "network of intentionalities," the "flow of experience," or the "interlocking intentionalities" through intentional analysis.[97] But there seems to be a provisional character about intentional analysis in the later works. This can readily be seen in chapter 5 of *The Visible and the Invisible* entitled "Preobjective Being: The Solipsist World."

In that section Merleau-Ponty remarks that the brute world "left intact by science and by reflection" invites an interrogation without presupposing anything.[98] The description of this domain is to be done without resort to the established contructs of science such as certain causal accounts of perception and without introducing into the description certain psychological or transcendental concepts issuing from reflection such as acts of consciousness, form, and perception.[99] That is to say, the description proceeds with cognizance of two precepts: 1) no recourse to established scientific constructs; and 2) no recourse to stock philosophical constructs.[100] But these precepts do not rule out the use of concepts in provisional ways. For Merleau-Ponty the expression "perceptual faith" is stipulated to mean "everything that is given to the natural man in the original in an experience-source with the force of what is inaugural and present in person, according to a view that for him is ultimate and could not conceivably be more perfect or closer." [101] In the event that the expression of this fundamental notion were misleading, one could "choose no interlocutor less compromising than *the whole of what is for us*" for purposes of elucidation.[102] Whatever the words selected for the expression of this concept, Merleau-Ponty is adamant in his conviction that philosophical interrogation can make use of concepts and should elucidate those least compromising in terms of the two precepts: "words being taken as simple indexes of a meaning to be specified." [103]

More importantly, such elucidations will be somewhat provisional in the sense that "if only in order to see these margins of presence, to discern these references, to put them to the test, or to interrogate them, we do indeed first have to fix our gaze on what is apparently *given* to us." [104] Thus, despite the fact that, as Claude Lefort notes, Merleau-Ponty would not have retained chapter 5, but would have replaced it with "Interrogation and Intuition" (chapter 3) in the finished manuscript, it seems that there are few doctrinal incompatibilities on the methodological primacy of reflection internal to *The Visible and the Invisible.*[105]

Moreover, there seems to be little doctrinal incompatibility between intentional analysis in the early works and in the later works. Further evidence of this interpretation lies in the frequency with which Merleau-Ponty uses a combination of "living the body" and "intentional analysis" even in the later works. For example, he writes: "I am a field of experience where there is only sketched out the family of material things and other families and the world as their common style, the family of things said and the world of speech as their common style, and finally the abstract and fleshless style of something in general." [106] Here it is not clear that he is making exclusive use of "living the body" or of "intentional analysis" in his descriptions. Rather, both seem to be at work at once. Both take cognizance of the crisscrossings of experience. Again he states: "It is a marvel too little noticed that every movement of my eyes—even more, every displacement of my body—has its place in the same visible universe that I itemize and explore with them, as, conversely, every vision takes place somewhere in the tactile space. There is double and crossed situating of the visible in the tangible and of the tangible in the visible; the two maps are complete, and yet they do not merge into one. The two parts are total parts and yet are not superposable." [107]

Perhaps for Merleau-Ponty it is not the case that "living the body" alone or "intentional analysis" alone suffices to elucidate the experience and concept of perceptual faith. Rather the combined procedures alone suffice. In that event, these combined procedures akin to "demonstrating the semantics of a word" and to "explaining the syntactics of a word" constitute for Merleau-Ponty his strong methodological view of the primacy of reflection. Certainly this is consistent with his confident assertion in *Themes from the Lectures* that through a study of linguistic symbolism "we shall be in a position to ascertain definitely the philosophical meaning of the preceding analyses, of the problem of the relation between 'natural' expression and cultural expression." [108] And it is consonant with his phenomenological positivism that linguistic symbolism often forgets its origins.[109]

5

Bernard Flynn

THE QUESTION OF ONTOLOGY
SARTRE AND MERLEAU-PONTY

IN THIS essay we will consider Merleau-Ponty's critique of Sartre's philosophy of negativity as presented primarily in *The Visible and the Invisible*. The political dimension of the friendship between Sartre and Merleau-Ponty, "that quarrel that never took place," [1] will be dealt with elsewhere in this volume.

For Merleau-Ponty, in *The Visible and the Invisible* as in the *Phenomenology of Perception*, the world of perception is a philosophical touchstone. The work of philosophy is to bring to expression the silent world of perception. Philosophy "is the experience . . . still mute which we are concerned with leading to the pure expression of its own meaning." [2] A philosophy will be judged in terms of its ability to "keep the faith," a faith established in perception before all philosophical reflection. As stated in the preface to the *Phenomenology*, "all its efforts are concentrated upon reachieving a direct and primitive contact with the world, and endowing that contact with a philosophical status." [3] Empiricism and analytic reflection either fall short of or overshoot the world. Empiricism falls short of the world by interposing a tissue of cultural artifacts— the concepts of sensations, reflex arc, etc.—between the perceiving subject and the world. Analytic reflection overshoots the world by dissolving it into the a priori conditions of its possibility. Analytic reflection thinks it can follow backward, to a constituting subject, the very path taken by this subject in constituting the world. This reflection would thus possess the key, the a priori of the world. It would "recuperate everything except itself as an effort of recuperation, it would clarify everything except its own role." [4] Reflection does not tell us why reflection is necessary, how mind becomes alienated and thus requires reflection. It lives parasitically from a contact with a real world, always already there, to which it does not address itself except in the form of the hypothetical, "if there is to be a world, then. . . ." However, there is a world and analytic reflection does not speak to our inherence in it. "The search for the conditions of possibility is in principle posterior to an actual experience, and from this it follows that even if subsequently one determines rigorously the *sine qua non* of that experience, it can never be washed of the original stain of having been discovered *post festum* nor ever become what positively founds that experience." [5]

The attraction of the philosophy of *Being and Nothingness* is its direct and immediate openness upon being. The philosophy of Sartre evicts all the inhabitants of consciousness—sense data, hyle, representations, psychological and transcendental egos. Consciousness, thought radically as negativity, precludes any form of opacity that would install itself between the subject and the world. Consciousness is the negation which opens a space in which being comes to appear "such as it is." Thus as Sartre states in his article on intentionality, consciousness is "in the dry dust of the world, upon the rude earth, among the things . . ." [6]

Unlike analytical reflection the philosophy of negativity does not attempt to found the being of the world. Consciousness which is its own negativity is cast upon the positive being of the world. The being of the world is not founded by consciousness. Being has no sufficient reason; it is radically contingent. One never arrives at the condition of its possibility. One can say of it only that it is. We will return later to the philosophy of negativity and analytic reflection.

According to Sartre, consciousness is its own appearance to self; all consciousness is consciousness (of) self, nonpositional self-consciousness, indicated by placing the *of* in *consciousness of self* in parenthesis. It is appearance to self by being the negation of itself. This system of internal negation, lest it fall into absolute nothingness, is directly cast upon the being of the world; it is a positional consciousness of something. The negativity of consciousness is our guarantee of an unmediated access to the being of the world, ". . . the For-itself is immediate presence to being and, at the same time, there slips in an infinite distance between itself and being." [7] This infinite distance is the nothingness of the For-itself, its refusal of being. It is this nothingness which disrupts the dark night of identity in which all cows are black. Negativity opens a clearing in which being comes to appearance "such as it is." Consciousness adds nothing; rather it opens a system of internal articulations through which an object can appear. Thus the philosophy of negativity accords with the article of perceptual faith according to which our cognitive life attains a direct access to the things themselves.

Only a thought which philosophically ratifies our prephilosophical conviction of achieving a presence to the world as it is, is capable of thinking an intersubjective world—a world accessible to and including other subjects as fully subject as myself. A philosophy which transposes the world into the contents of consciousness is incapable of achieving anything but an idea or a representation of the other and not the other person in flesh and blood. One would have to decide, or to judge as Descartes tells us, whether this representation is really a representation of another person, or whether it only refers to a robot dressed in hat and coat.

With regard to the intersubjective world and the being of the other, analytic reflection proves too much. Insofar as the transcendental ego is coextensive with the entire universe of meaningful being, the problem of communication is annulled by the ultimate identity of all thinking subjects: "In so far as I am a consciousness, that is, in so far as something has meaning for me, I am neither here nor there, neither Peter or Paul; I am in no way distinguishable from an 'other' consciousness . . ." [8] A thought which "gets below" our inherence in the world—our situation, our body—cannot define consciousness in individual terms; thus the collapse of the other into the self.

In the preface to the *Phenomenology*, Merleau-Ponty tells us in effect that if we have no "outside" the other has no "inside." "I must be the exterior that I present to others, and the body of the other must be the other himself." [9] Since the philosophy of *Being and*

Nothingness rejects any interior being or "inner life," the appearance of another subject is possible though not necessary. The For-itself, as we have seen, is nothing; it "is" only by being cast upon the being of the world. The For-itself "is" its situation. The appearance of the other, as Merleau-Ponty says, "takes my generosity at its word, it summons me to keep the promises I made when I admitted that I was *nothing* and that I was surpassed by being." [10] I discover the subjective being of the other through the experience of myself as object, as radically equated with my situation, with my body. I find the other by finding myself as a visibility, visible for the other but radically invisible for myself. It must be emphasized that I am what the other sees. The appearance of the other confirms what we have already seen—that I am my own exteriority. Beneath the look of the other there is neither escape nor excuse. I am what he sees. The existence of the other is not deducible from, nor necessitated by, my own existence; if it were, the other would be a dimension of my existence and would loose his alterity. The other is not merely a fact of my experience; his existence is given through the cogito. In my experience of myself as object, "the other is born *from my side* . . ." [11] The existence of the other is thus given with the same certainty as my own, and conversely participates in the same contingency.

All told, therefore, a rigorous philosophy of negintuition accounts for the private worlds without shutting us up in them: strictly speaking there is no intermundane space; each one inhabits only his own, sees only according to his own point of view, enters into being only through his situation. But because he is nothing and because his relationship with his situation and with his body is a relation of being, his situation, his body, his thoughts do not form a screen between him and the world; on the contrary they are the vehicle of a relation to Being in which third parties, witnesses, can intervene. [12]

We must turn now to Merleau-Ponty's critique of Sartre's ontology. The question is whether it is possible to think the appearance of the world, the apparition of being, in terms of the concepts of being and nothingness—in terms of a negation which decomposes the identity of being and opens a space in which being comes to appearance.

Merleau-Ponty writes in the preface to the *Phenomenology* that we must describe and not construct our relationship with the world. His fundamental objection to Sartre's philosophy of negativity is that it does not describe but constructs the openness of being through the concepts of being and nothingness. These concepts, arrived at prior to description, constitute the framework in which Sartre's description of our relationship with the world will be carried out. "The thought of the pure negative or of the pure positive is therefore a high-altitude thought, which operates on the essence or on the pure negation of the essence, on terms whose signification has been fixed and which it holds in its possession." [13] Furthermore, ". . . the dialectic of being and nothingness is only a preparation for experience . . ." [14]

For Merleau-Ponty, the philosophy of negativity is high-altitude thinking because the concepts that are used to explicate our inherence in the world are arrived at prior to a reflection on our inherence in being. Our experience is thus surveyed from above. No matter how "concrete" the situation described, whether it be sadomasochism or the project of giving up smoking cigarettes, the analysis is always generated in terms of the concepts of pure being and pure nothingness which precede all possible experience. Merleau-Ponty senses that in Sartre's philosophy the pure concepts of being and nothingness are everywhere and nowhere. Sartre insists that these concepts be thought in their purity. Nothingness is not a kind of being, a sort of ethereal subjectivity. Nothingness is not; it actively pursues its own negation. In its turn, being is thought in its purity. Sartre tells us that we can say of being only "that it is, that it is what it is and is not what it is not." However, when we turn to experience these concepts are never realized in their purity. Experience gives us mixtures, situations, and gradations. For Merleau-Ponty, the attempt to understand the fundamental openness of being in terms of the admixture of the pure concepts of being and nothingness is what constitutes Sartre's philosophy as high-altitude thinking. "We do not think then that the dichotomy of Being and Nothingness continues to hold when one arrives at the descriptions of nothingness sunken into being; it seems to us therefore that it is an abstract introduction to those descriptions . . ." [15] But if the dichotomy of being and nothingness does not hold at the level of experience (nothingness sunken into being), and if experience is our fundamental openness to being, then what is the justification for explicating experience through the pure concepts of being and nothingness?

If experience always gives us a nothingness already sunken into being, then from whence do the pure concepts of being and nothingness derive? To answer this question we must turn to the work of Sartre. Sartre arrives at the pure concepts of being and nothingness in his introduction to *Being and Nothingness*. The first thing to be noted about this introduction is that it does not proceed as a phenomenological description; it is a dialectical argument in the sense that Plato and Aristotle used the term. If one rejects the dualism of essence and appearance, and Sartre considers this the achievement of modern philosophy, then how is it possible to think the transphenomenal foundation of the being of appearance?

One must note that the "how is it possible" indicates a continuity between the philosophy of Sartre and the tradition of analytical reflection.

In this context, of course, we can only give a schematic outline of Sartre's argument. Sartre proceeds in true dialectical fashion. He proposes various possible solutions to the question of the transphenomenal being of appearance; he shows that each solution in its turn leads to conclusions which are either self-contradictory or absurd.

In the phenomena are not the outside shell of noumenal being that exists in-itself, and if appearances are relative to the subject to whom they appear, then it seems to follow that the phenomena are founded upon the being of the subject. It must be noted that the being of the phenomena is founded on consciousness as being, not as knowing. Otherwise the totality "knowing-known," would lack "the support of a solid being and so fall away in nothingness." [16] This leads us to the absurd conclusion that appearance is founded on non-appearance, that a process could found knowledge in complete ignorance of itself. Perhaps we could avoid this conclusion by describing knowledge as self-knowledge; but this would lead us into an infinite regress of "knowing-known" relations. Furthermore, it is in obvious contradiction with experience. We must discover trans-phenomenal being, a being which is not equal to our knowledge of it, on the side of consciousness, without being led into either of the two above absurdities. Sartre discovers this transphenomenality of consciousness in the prereflective cogito. All consciousness is a con-sciousness (of) self. Prereflective consciousness does not posit itself as an object; thus the parenthesis around the *of*. Nonetheless, it ex-ists as presence to itself. There is no logical distinction between pleasure and consciousness (of) pleasure, but there is no identity either. Consciousness is a noncoincidence with itself, a spontaneous presence to itself. It exists as a witness to itself, as For-itself. "Pres-ence is an immediate deterioration of coincidence, for it supposes separation." [17] It is nothingness that separates consciousness from itself. "The being of consciousness *qua* consciousness is to exist at a distance from itself as a presence to itself, and this empty distance which being carries in its being is Nothingness." [18] Thus by examin-ing the transphenomenality of the prereflective cogito, we arrive at the concept of nothingness.

Is this transphenomenality of consciousness capable of grounding the being of appearance? The prereflective cogito is a nonpositional consciousness (of) itself and a positional consciousness of something. However, the spontaneous inexistence of consciousness cannot be the foundation of the being of the "something." "The mode of the *percipi* is the passive." [19] Consciousness which is absolute trans-parency excludes all passivity and opacity, and thus cannot be the foundation of the passive "something" of which it is conscious. Nor can we use Husserl's concept of *hyle* as a mediation between the spontaneity of consciousness and the passivity of the perceived. Sartre says of the notion of *hyle* that it is a "hybrid being which consciousness rejects and which cannot be a part of the world." [20] Consciousness cannot be the foundation of the being of the world. On the contrary, the self-nihilation of the For-itself can exist (in-exist) only by being thrown upon the being of the world. The proc-ess of reflection-reflecting (perception-consciousness [of] perception) can inexist only by being the consciousness of something. "Con-sciousness implies in its being a non-conscious and transphenomenal being." [21] For Sartre, the being of consciousness as intentionality implies, but is not the foundation of, the being of the world.

Appearances are not based upon a thing behind the phenomena, but upon a being-in-itself, a being which overflows its phenomenality. "This meaning [appearance] has itself a being, based on which it manifests itself." [22] Of this being, on the basis of which the phenomena manifest themselves, we can only say: "it is full positivity." [23] "Being is. Being is in-itself. Being is what it is." [24] It is precisely what the For-itself is not.

The basic concepts of Sartre's philosophy are generated in his attempt to radically think through the concept of intentionality. Sartre's effort is to extricate the concept of intentionality from the constitutive idealism of Husserl.

Merleau-Ponty argues that these concepts, derived from a dialectical argument, are not adequate to think the event of the appearance of being. According to him, the negativist conception of consciousness generates a positivist conception of the world, "it is compensating for one abstraction with a counterabstraction." [25] Being becomes positive—full positivity; ". . . in every case it ignores density, depth, the plurality of planes, the background worlds." Merleau-Ponty continues, ". . . this being, in order to be positive and full, must be flat, and hence remains *what it is* beyond the ambivalence to which we are confined." [26] Merleau-Ponty calls the philosophy of negativity the principle of identity in action. Everything is what it is or is not what it is not. At this point his critique of Sartre's "positivism" rejoins his critique of the positivist ontology presupposed by empiricist psychology. The empiricist attempts to construct the perceptual field out of atomic sensations; each piece of sensation corresponds to a piece of the real world—the hypothesis of constancy. This hypothesis is disregarded by Merleau-Ponty because it is inadequate to the perceptual field which is crisscrossed with ambiguity, structured in depth and gradation. Things in the perceived world are not either present or absent; they are present in levels and gradations and their absence trails off gradually from the field of presence. "A visual field is not made up of limited views. But an object seen is made up of bits of matter . . ." [27] In the *Phenomenology*, Merleau-Ponty tells us that the empiricist's epistemology is motivated by a "prejudice of the world," an "obsession with being," or as we could say now the "principle of identity in action." Merleau-Ponty rejects all attempts to found the twisting, turning, or "intertwined" world of perception on being—fully positive and un-ambiguously present.

For Merleau-Ponty, the philosophy of *Being and Nothingness* coincides with a certain "madness" of the vision. "Through the holes of the eyes and from the bottom of my invisible retreat, I survey the world and rejoin it where it is." [28] From a certain perspective, the vision seems to emanate from a nothingness—a point of zero visibility—to the things fully in their place. But this vision which empties an absolute interval between itself and its object is a vision that forgets it has a body. Vision does not emanate from nowhere, but from a body which is itself visible. The word *vision* is itself equivocal; it signifies both the act of seeing and a thing seen.

Now we must contrast the concept of vision which motivates the philosophy of negativity, with the notion of vision elaborated by Merleau-Ponty in *The Visible and the Invisible*. Ultimately what we are considering are two different conceptions of the *Wessen* in its verbal sense—the how of being revealing itself. For Sartre, as we have seen, revelation is the work of negation; reversing Spinoza, "all determination is negation." To this philosophy of negativity, Merleau-Ponty opposes a philosophy of inherence. Being comes to presence not by negation but by a reversibility, an intertwining.

. . . because my eyes which see, my hands which touch, can also be seen and touched, because, therefore in this sense they see and touch the visible, the tangible, from within, because our flesh lines and even envelops all the visible and tangible things which nevertheless it is surrounded, the world and I are within one another, and there is no anteriority of the *percipere* to the *percipi,* there is simultaneity or even retardation.[29]

For Merleau-Ponty, being reveals itself not across an interval of nothingness, but from a profound intimacy of the body and the world, "as close as between the sea and the sand." [30] Between the body and the world there is "some relationship by principle, some kinship . . ." [31] The Sartrean notion of negativity is replaced by the concept of intertwining or reversibility. The body does not exist univocally. It is a being of two dimensions, "a being of two leaves, from one side a thing among things and otherwise what sees them and touches them." [32] The body is of the stuff of the world; it is a being of the same order—visible and tangible. It is the place of reversibility, a visible seeing and a tangible touching. The body is ultimately "neither thing seen only nor seer only, it is Visibility sometimes wandering and sometimes reassembled." [33] It is an archetype of the being of the visible because it is itself a being of plains and dimensions. We must not understand this theme of intimacy to pass over into a theme of identity. The reversibility of the visible and the seer, the touched and the touching, the objective body and the phenomenal body, is always in the process of happening, it is forever unachieved.

> . . . we spoke summarily of a reversibility of the seeing and the visible, of the touching and the touched. It is time to emphasize that it is a reversibility always imminent and never realized in fact. My left hand is always on the verge of touching my right hand touching the things, but I never reach coincidence; the coincidence eclipses at the moment of realization, and one of two things always occurs: either my right hand really passes over to the rank of touched, but then its hold on the world is interrupted; or it retains its hold on the world, but then I do not really touch *it*—my right hand touching, I palpate with my left hand only its outer covering.[34]

Life and thus the life of philosophy does not exist as a coincidence with being, but as an interrogation of being. A philosophy of coincidence, like a philosophy of negativity, would flatten the planes and dimensions of the *Lebenswelt*.

As we have seen above, Sartre arrives at the fundamental concepts of being and nothingness by a radical reflection on the concept of intentionality. In *The Visible and the Invisible,* the concept of intentionality or existence is replaced by the concept of reversibility. Merleau-Ponty writes of the body that "it is not in the world"; it does not "leave 'itself'." [35] The doubling of the sensible on itself is not adequately thought by the concept of the intentional act. The intentional act leaves itself to make itself present to a being of another order: the reality of the noesis—the irreality of the noema, the negativity of the For-itself—the positivity of the In-itself. We must remember that the concept of intentionality entered modern philosophy with Brentano's attempt to radically distinguish two orders of reality—the psychical and the physical. The vision, according to Merleau-Ponty, is fundamentally narcissistic. "Thus since the seer is caught up in what he sees, it is still himself he sees . . ." [36] More basically, since the seer and the seen are both moments of an elemental being, "a universal flesh," there is a reciprocity between the seer and the seen; ". . . we no longer know which sees and which is seen." [37] The openness of vision upon the visible is not achieved across a distance, but by a doubling of a universal flesh, the visible, upon itself. The concept of intentionality is no longer adequate to Merleau-Ponty's philosophical enterprise.

The ontology of being and nothingness constructs rather than describes our openness upon being. Our inherence in being, our destiny for being, is annulled when it is transposed into the concepts of a transparent nothingness and a fully positive and opaque being. In an analogous manner, Merleau-Ponty contends that Sartre's philosophy of negativity removes us from other people and the human world. According to Sartre, I do not discover another person, but only a dimension of myself that comes to be fixed through the other's look. In describing Sartre's philosophy of intersubjectivity we insisted that I am what the other sees; however, this implies that the other's presence adds nothing. The other only "freezes" me into what I have made of myself. ". . . his power over me is exactly measured by the consent which I have given to my body, to my situation; he has alienating force only because I alienate myself. Philosophically speaking, there is no experience of the other." [38] For Sartre, the other is "transcendence-transcending," an "ontological catastrophe" [39] who casts the seer into question,[40] or a "transcendence-transcended"—the other seen from "the heights of the towers of Notre-Dame." [41] In explaining Sartre's ontology, Merleau-Ponty uses the phrase "frontal being" to which he opposes his own concept of "field being." The paradigm for Sartre's philosophy of the other is direct confrontation; for Merleau-Ponty's philosophy it is the sense of always being already involved in a human world—an involvement which predates and subtends any explicit "frontal" encounter with another individual. ". . . he can look at me—me, the invisible—only because we belong to the same system of being for itself and being for another; we are moments of the same syntax, we count in the same world, we belong to the same Being." [42] According to Merleau-Ponty, our presence to the other is less an explicit event than a condition of our existence.

These differences regarding the notion of intersubjectivity become important in the political debate between Sartre and Merleau-Ponty concerning the role of a revolutionary party. In his article "Sartre and Ultra-Bolshevism," [43] Merleau-Ponty argues that Sartre recognizes the political existence of the proletariat only as explicitly expressed in the Communist party. The working class as an historical agent, a class for-itself, exists only insofar as its revolutionary aims are posited in opposition to the parties and the state of the bourgeois class. The importance granted to the party and the downgrading of the role of working-class spontaneity lead Merleau-Ponty to call Sartre's position "Ultra-Bolshevik."

For Merleau-Ponty, the historical being of a class is less the explicit positing of revolutionary goals than a shared intersubjective condition; ". . . the social exists obscurely and as a summons." [44] "The Russian peasants of 1917 joined the workers of Petrograd and Moscow in the struggle, because they felt that they shared the same fate; class was experienced in concrete terms before becoming the object of a deliberate volition." [45] In his article on Lukacs's conception of class and party, Merleau-Ponty writes, "Class consciousness is not, in the proletariat, a state of mind or knowledge. Nor is it a theoretician's conception. It is praxis, i.e., less than a subject and more than an object, a polarized existence, a possibility which manifests itself in the situation of the proletariat, at the juncture between things and his life: in brief . . . an 'objective possibility'." [46]

As seen by Merleau-Ponty, the philosophical project of Sartre's ontology is a reflection which reaches beyond, gets under, our inherence in the world and reconstructs our openness upon the world in terms of the pure concepts of being and nothingness. This reflection is total and radical.

Characterizing Merleau-Ponty's philosophical stance, Claude Lefort quotes Franz Kafka as saying that things give themselves "not by their roots, but by some point or other situated toward the middle of them." [47] Merleau-Ponty's reflection is indeed radical. He wishes to descend to a primitive contact with the world before the bifurcation of subject-object, nothingness-being. At the site of this primitive contact with the world rather than discovering generative principles or fundamental categories, we discover our insertion into "savage being" somewhere "toward the middle."

6

Joseph Bien

MERLEAU-PONTY'S CONCEPTION OF HISTORY

MERLEAU-PONTY did not develop a philosophy of history in the strict sense, for his aim was not so much to search out the meaning in history as it was to eliminate what was meaningless from it. At the core of this endeavor lay the conviction that man is eternally incomplete and that consequently his continual quest for absolute truth will never be brought to a successful conclusion. Inheriting the past actions of others, taking them up, and giving them new meanings in his present situation, man is both the curator of history and an actor in it. But while his scope of action as a curator is already defined, man as a historical actor can not only take up the givens of the past and add to them, but can also assign them new meanings. He is caught neither in the Heraclitean river nor in the atomistic conception of isolated present moments: he frees himself from the former through his individual action in the present, and from the latter in so far as he is an inheritor of the past.

To better understand what this means we must briefly refer to Merleau-Ponty's presentation of man's relationship to the world. While man as a subject has *this* body and no other, and so has his *particular* consciousness in distinction to some pure consciousness,[1] as subject he is inseparable from the world that his consciousness projects through his body. "The world is inseparable from the subject, but from a subject which is nothing but a project of the world, and the subject is inseparable from the world, but from a world that it projects itself."[2] To speak of a world existing prior to man is, for Merleau-Ponty, incomprehensible, if by such a statement one wishes to portray what the world may have been before man's entrance into it without referring to the world since man; the very language that is used in such a description is meaningful only to men already existing in the world. The body temporally defines man, places him in the world, and brings the lived past and possible future together in the awareness that the body-enclosed consciousness acquires of itself.

To have a body is to possess a universal setting. . . . the human body, with its habits which weave round it a human environment, has running through it a movement towards the world itself. . . . Human life is defined in terms of this power which it has of denying itself in objective thought, a power which stems from its primordial attachment to the world itself. Human life 'understands' not only a certain environment, but an infinite number of possible environments, and it understands itself because it is thrown into a natural world.[3]

But the world is never complete; it is a continual development in which the subject is able to transcend himself through his experiences with the world. "A world which, as Malebranche puts it, never gets beyond being an 'unfinished work,' or which, as Husserl says of the body, is 'never completely constituted,' does not require, and even rules out, a constituting subject." [4] The world is thus the unity of all men's actions, the very field on which each will play out his ambitions and desires.

In much the same way, time would have no past or future without there being an observer in the present. It is only through man's living in the present that a lived past and a possible future can be spoken of, and it is through the present that man as a subject can open onto a past and a still unlived future. As an essentially temporal being, man encounters in the present other subjects, other lived temporalities, and so can enter into the social. Just as man and the world project one another and are mutually inseparable, so also are men acting intersubjectively, and the present can be seen as the moment of intersubjectivity, the mediation between the individual and the general. Man's historical situation is his access to the world around him,[5] and he can neither escape nor speak from outside it. Yet he can give new meaning to it by projecting it into a future that will in turn take up this present (which will then be past) and so be oriented by it.[6] Just as the child finds himself in a natural world and appropriates the natural objects around him, so also he discovers a cultural world and appropriates its objects.[7] This may be clearly seen in the case of language. A dialogue takes place not between two objects or two subjects independent of one another, but intersubjectively: a world of discussion is shared by us, we have the common goal of carrying on this discussion in which we are both distinct participants but in which we find a common purpose. We are both recipients of a cultural inheritance, the given language, which directs us toward our social existence in order to participate in it and which allows us to create new meanings within it. The language is not something new and different at every moment, but is part and parcel of the particular consciousness of men situated in a particular historical moment. In turn man's situation is not something that is suddenly realized by him in an intellectual operation devoid of motive; [8] rather it comes from his very existence as a man. The fact that I consider myself bourgeois rather than proletarian is the result of having experienced and lived a certain situation and having come to the realization that I share this situation with others of my kind.[9] I realize this as my particular situation and may or may not act to change or continue it. At the same time I could not realize myself as either proletarian or bourgeois unless I was defining myself in relation to a larger social world, a situation shared by others. My individual situation is therefore part of a larger situation shared by other men in a given historical moment.

While the idea of situation never allows for an absolute freedom, by eliminating both bare consciousness and absolute determinism, it allows for the possibility of historical action. But in turn those situations that we choose to enter into as we come into an already constituted world so strongly entail our future choices that it is impossible to determine fully what is given by personal freedom and what is given by the situation. It is only through an intersubjective historical relationship that man is able to transcend himself. Man differs from the animals in that he projects his own situation in the world; he is not determined from the outside, for from the beginning he is directed to the world. He is a being sharing a common historical situation and as such is able to take up the meaning history presents to him and to give history its meaning through his actions.

History so conceived will have many possible meanings, for there is an exchange between the individual and the general. Through his free action man modifies history and gives it its significance in a particular world situation. This is how past action can be judged and the correctness of an action in the present assessed. Stalin may be viewed as an obscure Georgian who had the good chance and Machiavellian ability to become dictator of Russia or as a necessary instrument in the industrial development of the Soviet Union, or as both. How this is to be decided is the problem, for we will never have absolute certainty in historical matters, short of having absolute knowledge, of knowing all of history. To do so would mean that one was situated at the end of history, which is the same as the end of mankind.

Just as man develops his bodily well-being by acquiring certain habits and thus giving it direction, so also do men in their intersubjective actions take on common endeavors and give direction to their actions within history. But to point to the difficulty in speaking of the meaning of a given historical epoch is to point to an ambiguity in the term *history,* and perhaps in the very situation of man as a historical agent. The term *history* covers two different areas, referring on the one hand to historical reality and, on the other, to the study of history. The understanding of how these two things are related depends on how one understands man's relation to history. He is the inheritor and interpreter of history, but at the same time he himself is part of that history. Can man somehow transcend his existence as a historical agent to arrive at the position of objectively interpreting that of which he is a part? In his attempt to answer this question Merleau-Ponty turned to Max Weber and the early Marx as the principal exponents of the two most important modern explanations of man's place in history: capitalism and communism.

Max Weber accepted the dual roles of interpreter and agent in his examination of Protestant influences on capitalism. Realizing that a particular past only becomes historical when related to a particular present, Weber went to the sources of his present by studying Calvinism. He was able to do so, not because history has some unique meaning which is given to us through methodological examination, but rather because he could relate his own individual cultural experiences to those of past cultures by understanding the actions of other free cultural agents in history.[10] This is not to suggest that history is merely another subjectivity that depends on the present for its entire meaning. Weber was well aware of the alternative histories, one introducing arbitrarily chosen categories [11] and one viewing itself as a series of isolated and limited cultural moments. For Weber these alternatives amounted to a choice between the assessment and judgment of our past, even if the past was to be seen as no more than a reflection of the present, and meaninglessness or chaos. Either men belong to a "cultural order" [12] in which their choices tend to be complementary and "freedom recognizes other freedoms," [13] or else man is an isolated, essentially nonhistorical, nontemporal individual. Weber saw no real alternative except to assume the impossible task of the historian, all the while realizing that absolute objectivity or impartiality is beyond the scope of man. History is the intelligible recording of man's intersubjective actions. Man is not only what he is in the present moment, he is also what he will become, what he wants to become, and what he wants to have been. History does not begin and end with a given existence; history is universal; it is human history. For a given history to be acceptable it must be related to man's universal action, to his cultural action as a temporal, situated subject, acting out his existence in cooperation with his fellow men. In order to make past action intelligible and not a mere recording of actions laid back-to-back, as so many overlapping independent moments of the present, the historian must have a unifying theme which takes up the meaning that is in the historical facts and makes them significant to his present era.

Men express their individual thoughts through their actions, and men acting intersubjectively express their common or social actions through culture. This latter is best seen in the institutions that they construct in a given historical moment. Weber considered the most important cultural expression of recent history to be capitalism, and to better understand how man expresses himself in capitalism, he thus examined the origins of this system. The origins of capitalism were located by Weber in Calvinism, which with its view of man's severence from the eternal, represented a transition from external explanations of man's actions in the world and pointed man in the direction of being the meaning-giver of his own existence. Calvinism divorced man from God and held that man is worthy of nothing. There was no salvation for man to be found within the church, as salvation or damnation had already been determined by God. Having thus no way of confronting or understanding his relationship to the absolute, the Calvinist tried to create reason within his world; he organized things, placing them and himself in a certain order in an attempt to overcome the absolute anguish he felt concerning his own ultimate situation. He was not interested in pleasure, but rather in rationalizing, in categorizing, in making his situation intelligible. History acquired a new importance, for it had to reflect reason and be more than a mere reflection of some unknowable absolute. In these ways Calvinism tried to relate the different aspects of man's existence to some general theme and worked on the chaos that had resulted from the lack of understandable communication with the absolute. Driven from knowledge of the absolute, man bestowed significance on the commonplace, he created meaning from his working on nature, and this became an end in itself. Modern man arrived on the scene of history: to show his value he demonstrates that he can control nature around him, that he is master of his immediate situation. This demonstration takes the form of the amassing and controlling of worldly goods.

Thus capitalism came to concentrate on man's practical attempts to live in the world. Benjamin Franklin's advocacy of frugality, shrewdness, and hard labor as a response to man's life situation illustrates how wealth and trade had become ultimate ends in themselves by the mid-eighteenth century. Capitalism, dependent in its origins on Calvinism, had by Weber's time gone beyond it, taking up some of its themes and rejecting others; but it still was to be understood in terms of its origins in the Calvinist dilemma. Capitalism was thus an advance in history, for it led man to come to grips with his own situation instead of looking for an answer to his problems in some definition of himself that takes him beyond the world. Yet it has lost the element of the transcendent that previously existed, and man has come to be defined in terms of what he has amassed. No one knows what tomorrow may bring, for history is contingent, but there does exist a measure for ordering the world: economic production.

Weber allowed us to look into our past and understand the origins of our present, thus fulfilling the role of the historian; but what of his role as an actor in the present? The present is a two-way street: on the one hand our present is shaped by our past, and we conceive our situation in terms of what has gone before; but the present is bidirectional, pointing not only toward the past in reference to its origins, but also to the future, thus defining itself in terms of its present aims. Our present situation also demands realization in a possible future. Weber, the man, can do no more than keep open an "affinity of choices" [14] for the future. As a historical actor he gives us not immanent historical rationalization but rather pluralism. He has pointed up the importance of the economic in man's past and present relationships, but he has shed no light on its relation to future developments. Weber might best be seen as a historian par excellence rather than as a historical actor who can give limit to the past through his action in the present situation. In this sense Weber is a liberal; he understands his origins and his relationship to the present without being able to realize the present as it is defined by a contingent future. He has shown us the need for reason in history, he has, in fact, pointed to the origins of a philosophy of history, but one in which we can only align ourselves without finding direction for the future. He has shown us the origins of the rationalization of our society in the Calvinist dilemma and in the perverted practice of its stepchild, capitalism; but for the future development of man's attempt to make history rational, one must look elsewhere. In this case Merleau-Ponty turned to Marx.

Merleau-Ponty's interest in Marxism was nothing haphazard, but rather resulted from his own situation in history. Marxism had gained great prestige in France through the Communist party's active participation in the underground movement during the Second World War, while at the same time much of the French Right had been discredited through either collaboration with the German occupation or lack of participation in the resistance to it. While Marxism and communism did not always present a united view of man, it was possible to see them as two aspects, Marxist theory and Communist practice, of an ongoing intersubjective history in which man's present historical situation was defined both by his inherited past and by his understanding of a possible future. It is easy enough to see how Merleau-Ponty, reflecting the spirit of his age, was concerned with this form of intersubjectivity manifested in Marxism and Communist action.

For Merleau-Ponty, to accept Marxism meant to answer three questions: 1) how was one to understand Marx's statement that man does not have an essence independent of the material conditions of his existence? 2) how was one to understand Marx's claim that the proletariat is the historical vehicle whereby man's recognition of man will be realized? and 3) how was the proletariat to become conscious of the role it is supposedly destined to play? To answer the first question required an understanding of historical materialism different from the then common presentation of it.

The view most commonly advanced in Marxism is that classes are defined by the relations of infrastructure and superstructure. This is to say that the objects of production (infrastructure) continually reflect the modifications of the relations of production, which are dialectically linked to such features of the superstructure as politics, religion, and law. It is through the different levels of class struggle that history's meaning emerges. This meaning is seen in the contradictions that emerge between the infrastructure and the superstructures of a given society, as they are dialectically allied to the consciousness that classes have of themselves.[15]

The question for Merleau-Ponty became one of showing how Marx gave an independent role to the superstructures, instead of making them mere reflections of the economic base of society. To do this he drew heavily on the writings of the young Marx and especially on the *1844 Manuscripts,* which began to receive serious attention from the French Left only in the postwar period. In these writings he found a Marx who viewed man's role as a historic being in much the same way he did. This young Marx was much concerned with overcoming the subject-object duality through the presentation of man as an intersubjective being. Merleau-Ponty laid emphasis on this humanist Marx by combating what he considered to be a mistaken interpretation of what Marx was doing.

What lends credibility to the legend of a Marxist positivism is that Marx is fighting on two fronts. On the one hand, he is opposed to all forms of mechanistic thought; on the other, he is waging war with idealism. . . . Marx. . . . would not even agree to speak of a collective consciousness whose instruments are individuals. . . . The individual is *social being.* Man is "a being which exists for itself," thus, a *generic being.* . . . [Man] is not in society as an object is in a box; rather he assumes it by what is innermost in him. This is why one can say that "man produces man himself and other men." "As society itself produces man as man, so it is produced by him." [16]

In such a view of Marxian materialism man is still at the center of the world, taking it up and giving it new meaning through his actions. Marx's importance for Merleau-Ponty was not in his emphasis of the economic base of society, but rather in his vision of man's problems as reflected in the economic.[17] The economic cannot be fully separated from the political and the religious. Rather all these social structures are united in social situations, though in a given moment reference to one of these factors may most economically explain a cultural or historical situation. In times of revolution, for example, it may well be that man's relationships can best be seen through his society's economic structures. But this is not to say that the objective economic conditions of a given society will always lead to a heightened level of class consciousness and possible revolution. One only has to look at history and observe the present world to see many cases of extreme economic deprivation without a corresponding class awareness. Class consciousness comes about through man's lived experience, through his coexistence with his fellow men, and through his understanding of his relation to other men who share his situation. Historical materialism rests neither on idealistic thought nor solely on the objective conditions. Decision cannot by itself bring class consciousness into being. Class, and the possibility of class consciousness, is present in capitalism not as something to be decided upon, but as something to be lived. The worker understands his class situation from a gradual lived experience with his fellow workers. He does not decide in one moment that he is a member of the proletariat, for such a decision would imply that there is already an immediate answer contained in the question, that the decision can be reached now, once and for all; in short, that his nature, arising from his historical situation, is fixed in much the same way as the liberal theoreticians' conception of rational man as ahistorical. To believe that class is determined by such decisions would be to revert "to immanence and abandon the attempt to understand history." [18] The coming to be of class consciousness is ultimately an "existential project." [19] Economics is thus not to be seen as the determinant of man's social situation, but as an essential element in understanding man's direction in the world.

Such a view of historical materialism as Merleau-Ponty proposes to us reflects the entire realm of man's activities. It admits of the infrastructure's essential role in society, which is itself in situation in history, since men's actions are not explainable outside of their situation in an economic system of production. In much the same way that man projects his world while being a projection of it, he is at the center of his intersubjective relations and reflects his economic origins in his actions to the extent that they aid him in understanding his present situation. Historical materialism so conceived goes beyond the traditional narrow interpretation of economics and bases history on more general styles of existing, rather than solely on a discussion of production and labor. Thus the historical materialism of the young Marx (as seen by Merleau-Ponty) emphasizes the dialectical relations of human practice and insists on man being the motive force in history. Merleau-Ponty finds that in Marx, "For the first time since Hegel, militant philosophy is reflecting not on subjectivity but on intersubjectivity." [20] History has taken on an understandable meaning without neglecting man's place at its center. According to this theory, history is neither "a series of juxtaposed 'self-consciousness' " [21] nor the perpetual domination of the economic; rather it sees ". . . that economic problems and cultural or human problems are a single problem, and that the proletariat, as history has shaped it, holds the solution to that problem." [22] If one accepts that it is in work, in the widest sense of the word, that man's dual relationship with nature and his fellowmen comes to concrete reality, one sees that "each system of production and of property implies a system of relationships among men of the sort that our relations with others are read in our relations with nature and our relations with nature in our relations with the other." [23]

The answer to Merleau-Ponty's second question—how the proletariat is the historical vehicle whereby man's recognition of man will be realized—demands a brief reference to Marx's criticism of Hegel's view of the role of the state and of its universal class of civil servants. In the *Philosophy of Right* Hegel arrived at the final stage of his historical movement of history, the state. It is in this final stage that the subject-object duality is supposedly overcome. In the previous stage of society, civil society, one saw the various interests at war with one another. Only with a universal class, the civil servant class, is it possible for these various interests to be reconciled and made mutually comprehensible. The universal class of civil servants participate in civil society as individual members, but with their established pensions they are removed from its conflicting economic interests and through training supposedly they are brought to realize the best interests of mankind. Thus according to Hegel this universal class acts for all mankind in individual decisions. Marx questioned the correctness of this view for at least two reasons, the most important being that the state is not an adequate representation of man's interactions, that it is in fact nothing more than the vehicle whereby the dominant class in a society controlled the dominated classes and carried out its aims. Such, according to Marx, had been the history of mankind's experience with the State. Hegel's civil servants would thus be dependent on whatever class was in power and would merely be second-level executives for the ruling class in civil society. The state, far from being the collapse of the subject and object, would be the historical representation of the subject-dominated object in its most extreme form. Consequently the liberal notion of equality in law and opportunity is not realized in pre-Communist societies. Merleau-Ponty comments: "Marxism shows that a politics based upon man in general, the citizen in general, justice and truth in general, once it is inserted into the concert totality of history, works to the advantage of very particular interests, and it focuses its criticism on these relations." [24] Marx pointed to the proletariat in capitalist societies as the first potentially universal class. It is potentially universal for two reasons: on the one hand, because of its particular place in the production process it has become "a sphere of society which has a *universal character* because its *sufferings are universal,* and which does not claim a PARTICULAR REDRESS because the wrong which is done to it is not a PARTICULAR WRONG but WRONG IN GENERAL"; [25] and, secondly, since the proletariat is the producer of all wealth in capitalist societies but receives only a minimal portion of it in return, once it comes to power it cannot produce another class to be exploited. With the present stage of capitalism, history has presented us with the first real possibility of man's overcoming the subject-object duality, through the potentially universal class, the proletariat. Merleau-Ponty stressed here the dependency to be found in the proletariat. It is because of the proletarian's particular situation under capitalism that he is free to see himself detached from this society and, at the same time, to be aware of his absolute dependence.[26] "For the proletariat individuality or self-consciousness and class consciousness are absolutely identical." [27] The proletarian case is that of the only true coexistence among men, and proletarian society is the true historical hope for a fully human society. Through the proletariat history has presented us with concert "universal individuals" in place of men separated by nationalism or religion.[28] "The proletariat . . . is the sole authentic intersubjectivity because it alone lives simultaneously the separation and union of individuals." [29]

Marx thus alerted us to the historical possibility of overcoming the present subject-object conflict and of realizing man in a more perfect form of intersubjectivity; as he said, the proletariat allows us to move from prehistory to a true history of mankind.[30] How this is to be done involves Merleau-Ponty's third question, the practical question of the coming to be of proletarian class consciousness. History has presented us with its historical actor, but has only hinted at the way the proletariat will realize itself. What we have been speaking of until now is the limit case of the proletariat, or the proletariat as it is generally seen in particular capitalist societies. Merleau-Ponty takes as his particular example the historical instantiation of the proletariat as seen in the Western world's clearest example, Russia. He agrees with Lenin and Marx that, while history is a system which demands the development of a world proletariat, this very development must be realized through specific cases; so one aspect or one country must be emphasized at a given moment. Following Marx, Lenin also realized that between the pure proletarian and the pure bourgeois there are many gradations, and that at any given moment the proletariat may well need guidance to come to consciousness of its correct action. For this a party is needed, and in demanding a party a subjective element is reintroduced into history. How the proletariat, the historical vehicle whereby man's recognition of man is to take place, and the party, which is to lead it to this recognition, relate to one another is a question left unresolved by Marx. Lenin suggests in places that the party be one of iron, in other words that it *lead* the proletariat to consciousness of its mission. If this be the case, is not the party acting as the subject of history and treating history's supposed vehicle merely as an object to be used for its own best interests? To justify such a position would require a knowledge of the end of history, but this would deny man as the center of an intersubjective history.

In an attempt to resolve this dilemma, Merleau-Ponty turned to the Hungarian philosopher Georg Lukács, and especially to his work *History and Class Consciousness*. Lukács saw the party as the historical instrument whereby, through a form of dual mediation, an already existing proletarian *praxis* which has not yet been brought to consciousness is realized. On the one hand the party mediates between the proletariat and history, and, on the other, it consults with the proletariat—which is another way of saying that the proletariat enters into a mediation between the party and history. The two form what Merleau-Ponty calls an "exchange between workers, who are also articulate men able to assimilate the theoretical views offered to them, and theoreticians, who are also living men capable of transposing into their theses what others experience." [31] It is easy enough to understand why this position was not accepted by the Russian party and why Lukács found himself in the embarrassing position of having to qualify and retract parts of what he had said in *History and Class Consciousness.* For from his view of dual media-tion one might reasonably conclude that, if the proletariat's role is to be taken seriously, the party has limited and contingent value in relation to the historical mission. Rather than being the necessary bridge beyond trade-unionism, as Lenin had suggested, the party now becomes farsighted members within the proletariat explaining their role to fellow proletarians. By silencing Lukács, the party effectively collapsed the second mediation into the first and insisted on Lenin's conception of the party as the actual historical mani-festation of world proletarian power. But in so doing they presented the party as the all-knowing and final arbiter of history; in effect they unknowingly claimed a knowledge of the end of history.

In replacing the dialectical relationship among men and things with a form of materialism, the dialectic is preserved only "by em-balming it outside us in an external reality";[32] the intersubjective role of man in history is lost, and all history can be read by the initiated. "The proletariat is displaced by the professional revo-lutionary, and history as well as cognitive movements are concen-trated in a fixed mechanism."[33] The proletariat that history has presented us as the vehicle whereby man's intersubjective existence is to be realized is thus shown to be deficient as the representation for the present historical moment, for it results in either a subjective history determined by its leaders (a variation on the great man theory of history), or it claims to place man outside history, or at best to use him in its realization as an object led by those who for unknown reasons are able to correctly grasp the determining factors of historical movement. Either conception of history would be a denial of the existential view of history that Merleau-Ponty ad-vanced. After a more detailed reading of the later writings of Marx, Merleau-Ponty rejected the Marxist interpretation of history, hold-ing that Marx in his later writings had passed from his earlier humanism to a positivistic variant of the dominance of the structures of a given society. Man as an agent was thereby reduced to filling the roles given to him by the economic structures of society.[34]

Considering the fact that Merleau-Ponty was one of the first French philosophers to appreciate the importance of Claude Lévi-

Strauss,[35] it may not be too great an exaggeration to suggest that in *Les aventures de la dialectique,* written in the early 1950s, he foresaw and rejected the turn Marxist criticism was to take in the 1960s under Louis Althusser and other members of the structuralist school.[36] When speaking of the dialectic in action, Merleau-Ponty says,

> If the revolutionary function of the proletariat is engraved in the infrastructure of capital, the political action which expresses it is justified, as the Inquisition, by providence. By presenting itself as the reflection of that which is, of the historical process in-itself, scientific socialism puts in the foreground the knowledge that *The Theses on Feuerbach* subordinated. It gives itself the right of an absolute knowledge and at the same time it authorizes itself, through violence, to take out of history a sense which is there, but surely deeply hidden.[37]

To discount Marx's view of history is not to negate all that Marx advanced, but rather it is to realize that the proletariat that Marx claims history proposes to us is not the solution of the present historical situation of man. It is possible, as Merleau-Ponty points out, that it may become the correct expression of man's existence in another situation at some future present.

Having put aside the Marxian philosophy of history, Merleau-Ponty in his later writings returned to Max Weber's work. In his lectures at the Collège de France[38] Merleau-Ponty reexamined the concept of pluralism and found in it the possibility of a unified interpretation of history that could show how the economic order interacts with politics, religion, etc., without setting up some external knowledge of history. Man is continually questioning the past in order to understand his own totality, and in so doing he realizes an "affinity of choices" in the present. "Man is a historian because he belongs to history, and history is only the amplification of practice."[39] History will itself always be fragile and contingent, for man at any moment in the present is always in development; the meaning that he receives from history at any time will be significant for his age and, inasmuch as both past and present belong to the unique and multireflectional realm of culture, it will have meaning for man in every age. "It is . . . through an unending interrogation that all the ages together compose a single and universal history." [40]

If, as Merleau-Ponty claimed, both the conservative and the revolutionary categories of history are bankrupt, man still remains at the center of meaning in history. While through recent technological and scientific discoveries, man's very relationship to the world may be in question—we have now been presented with energies beyond the framework of our world, energies which may be used to destroy the world we live in,[41] in much the same way that communism proposed a party which was somehow beyond human history, outside our conception of temporality, negating man coexistence while supposedly leading him to a more perfect intersubjectivity, —man still finds himself at the center of what he has created and, as a historical actor, is faced with the continuing need to give meaning to his experience, however ambiguous it may be,[42] to give direction to this world which he projects and of which he is both a historical and a spatial projection.

7

Dick Howard

AMBIGUOUS RADICALISM: MERLEAU-PONTY'S INTERROGATION OF POLITICAL THOUGHT

IT IS perhaps better to speak of political *interrogations,* and of an interrogation of the political, than to speak of political theory. What distinguishes the theories in the contemporary political arena is not what is said but what is left unsaid; it is not the problems solved but those evaded or hidden under sweeping slogans that measure the inadequacy of political thought to the modern world. Veiled in a rhetoric of positivity, political theory becomes a secular religion: a pragmatism that reifies and deifies the weight of facticity, or a faith in the mission of the proletariat (or the Third World, the Oppressed and Exploited . . .),—or a skepticism tinged with cynicism. The role of the critical intellect today is to return to the human soil which is the foundation, mediation, and end of politics. This return, whose means are its end, whose subject is its object, is not the work of an abstract or transcendental observer; it is the interrogation of the world by one who is in that world, the questioning of the other in the self and the self in the other. It is here that phenomenology has a contribution to make to radical political thought.

The first step in a radical reevaluation is to question the rationality on which politics bases itself. The pretended objectivity of theory, its quantative bias, and the separation of subject (observer) and object (observed) must be called into question. The pretentions of humanism and other forms of apriorist *hubris* are to be rejected, for politics is not the realm of abstract morality, and its subjects are not pure egos but embodied men and women living in an historically given socioeconomic and cultural world. The nature of the subject, its relation to the others who coconstitute society, and the social constitution of a history which is lived and made are questions which, though they at first seem abstract, cut to the heart of the pretensions of political theory.

This political interrogation constitutes the horizon of Merleau-Ponty's philosophical development in a twofold sense. The Marxian theory—and its Communist reformulation and implementation— were not simply the practical backdrop on which the engaged French intellectual had to trace a form; Merleau-Ponty's theory itself, from his earliest to his final works was informed by Marxism to perhaps the same degree as by Husserl's phenomenology. But Merleau-Ponty's technique was not simply to study or make use of a pregiven doctrine: he molded it to his own concerns, to the point that— though, as will be seen, he was not conscious of it—the interrogation begun by Marx became inseparable from his own. This is not to say that Merleau-Ponty was a Marxist, but only this: the style of his interrogation, the structure of his concerns, and his rootedness in lived experience make a contribution to the radical politics whose most important thinker has been Karl Marx.

In the love-hate relation between existentialism and Communist Marxism after the war, Merleau-Ponty's philosophical contribution was of far greater subtlety than that of Sartre, and Sartre admits that, during its early years, *Les Temps Modernes* was in fact directed by Merleau-Ponty. One need only compare Sartre's "Materialism and Revolution" with Merleau-Ponty's work during the same period: where Sartre was confronting established communism, Merleau-Ponty was interrogating Marx. While Sartre attacked the Communists' materialism for its neglect of the subject, Merleau-Ponty recognized that the progress of Marx over previous philosophies was precisely the dialectical interrelation it demonstrated between subject and object. He writes, for example, that "Marxism is not a philosophy of the subject, but it is just as far from a philosophy of the object: it is a philosophy of history." [1] It is here, insists Merleau-Ponty, that Marxism and phenomenology converge: both "introduce . . . the notion of the *human object.*" [2] The concern with the dialectic of subject and object, rejecting the traditional realist/ idealist option, is a major theme of *The Phenomenology of Perception*. Merleau-Ponty's phenomenological notion of "existence" runs in the same direction as the Marxian interpretation of "praxis," as is clear when he cites Husserl to the effect that "consciousness is originally not an 'I think that,' but an 'I can.' " [3] When he asks himself the question, "Isn't it necessary to choose: either the drama of coexistence has a purely economic signification, or the economic drama dissolves into a more general drama and has only existential signification . . . ," Merleau-Ponty replies that "If it is correctly understood the notion of existence permits us to go beyond precisely that alternative." [4]

The dialectical view of the subject—be it Hegel's "substance as subject," Marx's "praxis," or Merleau-Ponty's "existence"—is central for philosophy in general and to the political interrogation in particular, for it flies in the face of the categories of bourgeois common sense. There are no "subjects" and there are no "objects"; there is only a world which we cohabit with other persons and things, changing it and being changed by it. Because I am embodied, living in a world, my subjectivity is also an object, for others and even—in some revealing instances—for myself. This is why Marx's *Capital* is not a textbook in political economy but a theory of life in capitalist society. Merleau-Ponty's devastating refutation of Koestler's mechanistic opposition of the "Yogi" (Subjectivity) and the "Commisar" (Objectivity) clearly shows that the Marxian dialectic does not permit such a polarization and—since it is not simply a question of showing Koestler's misunderstanding of Marx—that a nondialectical view does not permit an understanding of the facts in question. The line of argument in *Humanism and Terror* is, it should be stressed, a continuation and elaboration of the viewpoint at which Merleau-Ponty arrived in *The Phenomenology of Perception*.

"Subject" and "object," "*Pour-Soi*" *and "En-Soi,"* are abstract oppositions whose very abstractness prevents an understanding of the rich texture of experience. A moral or political theory built on them will be like that of the bourgeoisie: principles are raised to the status of absolutes, but as abstract absolutes they serve as a spiritual cloak covering naked relations of exploitation and violence. The "liberty" and "equality" which bourgeois morality preaches are empty words in a class society, and for this reason Merleau-Ponty agrees with the Communists that change is needed. The problem is not whether violence is necessary for this change; Merleau-Ponty is concerned to find a violence which recedes with use, which negates the conditions for its employment. The proletarian revolution according to Marx is such a self-negating violence, for it will put an end to the society based on classes. But with what kind of necessity are we dealing when we say that this proletarian revolution is historically necessary? How, in other words, are we to account for a dialectical necessity without returning to the abstractness of the subject/object dichotomy, making revolution either a mechanistic necessity inscribed in things, or a moral Ought said somehow to be binding on "true subjectivity"?

Concomitant with the dialectical interplay and interdetermination of subject and object comes the notion of history, itself situated neither on the side of the subject nor that of the object. In *Humanism and Terror,* Merleau-Ponty exposes two possible and mutually exclusive radical approaches to history. "To be a revolutionary," he writes, "is to judge that which is in the name of what is not yet, taking it for more real than the real," for "revolutionary justice takes as its standard the future." [5] Implicit in this view is a kind of rationalism for which history is an object to be analyzed by a non-situated (transcendental) observer who can read the sense of history's direction without, by his reading, inflecting it. This view, which Merleau-Ponty criticizes as "Trotsky's rationalism," can be used as well for a theological politics of the progress toward the city of God as it can for a leftist position. Moreover, this is not the Marxian position:

Marxism is completely based on the idea that there is no such thing as destiny, that sociological "laws" are valid only within the framework of a certain historical state of society, that it is up to men to regain control of the social apparatus and change a history that is undergone into one that is willed; . . . Marxism consequently assumes a view of history which sees it as open, of man as maker of his fate.[6]

The dialectical view of history—that it can only be understood as lived, that the observer is situated within history—is fully consistent with Merleau-Ponty's previous analyses of perception, and he stresses this in *Humanism and Terror,* writing that Marxism "wanted to provide a *perception of history* which at each moment would make the lines of force and the vectors of the present appear."[7]

Merleau-Ponty's interrogation of history stresses the role of the participant in the structuration of contingency.

> History is there where there is a logic *within* contingence, a reason *within* unreason, where there is a historical perception which, like perception in general, leaves in the background what cannot enter the foreground but seizes the lines of force as they are generated and actively leads their traces to a conclusion. . . . all symbolic systems — perception, language, history — only become what they were, although in order to do so they need to be taken up into human initiative.[8]

This approach explains what Sartre calls Merleau-Ponty's "obstination in always digging at the same place," [9] as well as his opposition to the theory of art implied by Malraux's *Musée Imaginaire.* For him, "history is no longer a tête-à-tête between a Kantian understanding and a past in itself; understanding now discovers in its object its own origins." [10] History is multifaceted and open-ended, like the perceptual object that the artist — all artists — tries to penetrate through a ceaseless interrogation. This is why, in the incomplete and sometimes puzzling *Visible and the Invisible,* Merleau-Ponty continually speaks of "vertical Being," of "savage Being," and proposes a "transcendental geology" whose task would be the reactivation of the sedimented present.

The increasingly evident ineptitude of orthodox communism to cope with the problems of the cold war and colonial revolutions led Merleau-Ponty to rethink his views on Marxism in *Adventures of the Dialectic.* Aside from its lengthy polemic with Sartre, this book marks a date in the intellectual history of Marxism, reintroducing the most sophisticated and radical work in Marxist philosophy since Marx: Georg Lukács's *History and Class Consciousness.*[11] After tracing the history of Western Marxism, whose high point is Lukács's book, Merleau-Ponty concludes that the hope on which this philosophy was based has proven false. He admits that the class struggle still exists, and considers Marxism still valid as a critique and as an

heuristic method, but thinks that "revolutions are true as movements and false as regimes." [12] His conclusion is a strong condemna-
tion of left-wing optimism, and a call for the formation of a new,
consciously reformist left.

Leaving aside Merleau-Ponty's practical political suggestions,[13]
his critique of communism and Marxism poses important problems
which are still very much alive today. For Western Marxism, "The
revolution was that *sublime point* at which the real and values, the
subject and the object, judgement and discipline, the individual and
the totality, the present and the future, instead of entering into col-
lision gradually entered into complicity." [14] This formulation is
nothing but the consistent dialectical theory of revolution: neither
the result of objective evolution nor of subjective will, revolutionary
action occurs at the junction of project and projection, as Alfred
Willener puts it in his analysis of May 1968 in France.[15] Revolution
is not an accident, any more than is the work of art; but its necessity
is rooted in the contingency of history in the same way that not every
work of the artist can be called art. Like the work of art, revolution
is a timeless and therefore omnitemporal present in which the past
and the future, the subject and the object, the individual and the
world fuse. This explains why "revolutions are true as movements
and false as regimes," and poses the question: can the "sublime
point" be maintained or continually re-created? And in the case of
the latter option, does the force that recreates it remain a part of the
contingent totality, itself influenced by what it influences?

We have to shake ourselves loose from the "neurosis of the future," [16] and recognize that "history is not an external god, a hidden
reason whose conclusions we would only have to record," for "the
same life—our own—plays in us and outside of us, in our present
and in our past." [17] This is the central lesson of Western Marxism.
"The old problem of the relation of subject and object is transformed . . . once it is posed in terms of history, for here the object
is nothing but the traces left by other subjects, and the subject—
historical understanding—when taken within the tissue of history
is for this reason capable of self-criticism." [18] In other words, the
Darwinist Marxism of the Second International, as well as its Russian continuation as the positivist "dialectics of nature," are in fact

nondialectical and non-Marxist positions. In both, the subject is separated from and opposed to the object, following the model of positive science, with the result that history is said to obey pregiven laws, the subject is given no room for free action, the element of (class) consciousness is undervalued, and socialism is equated with the transformation of the economic base. On this basis one can establish a positive correspondence between the so-called infrastructure and superstructure, reducing the latter to a manifestation of the former and calling this an explanation. But, as Merleau-Ponty notes, this "frequently celebrated relationship between ideology and economy remains mystical, prelogical and unthinkable insofar as ideology remains 'subjective,' economy is conceived as an objective process, and the two are not made to communicate in the total historical existence and in the human objects which express it." [19] The dialectical view must stress contingency in a history whose objects are also its creators who, as object-subjects, can choose among the possibilities offered by a history which their choice coconstitutes.

The ambiguity which permits Marxists to make positive nondialectical claims has its origin with Marx, as Merleau-Ponty recognizes. ". . . to say with Marx that man only poses those problems that he can resolve is to renew theological optimism and to postulate the completion of the world." [20] There is a tendency in Marx, accentuated by the stress on "scientific socialism" and in the works of Engels, to see a directionality in history, to postulate a Truth toward which History must move, and to lose sight of the dialectical contingency in favor of a "voluntarism based on absolute knowledge." [21] This ambiguity makes itself felt in the tradition of Western Marxism itself, and accounts in part for the change in Lukács's position after 1923.

The problem is to maintain the dialectical contingency, to resist the temptation inherent in any revolutionary venture of taking one's politics as the expression of History. The key contribution of Western Marxism is its recognition of the importance of subjectivity, of the action of the proletariat, or, as Merleau-Ponty puts it, that "a politics 'for the people' which is not developed 'by the people' in the end is not developed at all . . . " [22] It must be recalled that Western Marxism grew up in the wake of the Russian Revolution

—though its origins in fact are in Rosa Luxemburg—which to its contemporaries appeared to be precisely that "sublime point" where the subjective will and the objective conditions come together and explode a past ripe with the future. Because the first socialist revolution took place in an underdeveloped country it was natural that revolutionary will would be stressed more than material conditions. Moreover, the zigzag course of the early years of the revolution and the political skills of Lenin, pointed out the importance of recognizing the contingencies of history and acting in terms of them.

With the death of Lenin and the consolidation of the revolution in Russia and its failure in the West, ideological hegemony within the Third International fell to the Bolsheviks, with disastrous results. Lukács's *History and Class Consciousness* and Korsch's *Marxism and Philosophy* were condemned in the same breath with Hegel's *Logic;* and Lenin's incredibly mechanistic *Materialism and Empirio-Criticism,* along with the theory of the dialectics of nature, was canonized. More importantly, the Leninist theory of the party was forced upon the members of the Third International. Significantly, Merleau-Ponty takes this theory of the party as the center of Marxism.[23] Hence, when he shows that "the absolute authority of the Party is nothing but the purity of the transcendental subject incorporated in the world by force," [24] he thinks that he has refuted Marxism. It is here that his analysis goes astray.

The Leninist theory of the party, which, in fact, has its roots in the German Social Democrat Karl Kautsky and also in the concrete conditions of Czarist Russia, is based on the assertion that in its day-to-day struggles at the workplace, the class can gain only "trade-union consciousness" which centers not around the seizure of political power but simply around "economist" struggles. For this reason, it is necessary that the proletariat gain political (class) consciousness from outside, from the party, which is viewed as the incarnation of the consciousness of the slumbering giant. As Merleau-Ponty reformulates it: "In philosophical terms: the party goes beyond the revolt of the proletariat; it realizes that revolt by destroying it as an immediate revolt; it is the negation of that negation, or in other words, it is the mediation, its action is such that the class which refuses becomes the class which founds and, finally, a society without classes." [25] The class is both subject and object of history: it is the product of capitalist conditions and relations of production, but at the same time it is the producer and reproducer of those conditions. The proletariat must put the two sides together, becoming conscious not simply of its immediate economic oppression but more—and this is what distinguishes a revolutionary movement from reformist trade-unionism—knowing that its immediate exploitation is mediated by an entire system of social and political relations which must be destroyed if the proletariat is to be free and to create a free society without classes. But, *ex hypothesis,* the Leninist theory postulates that the spontaneous revolts of the proletariat are only economist, unaware of the social totality; hence, the party is needed as the mediation.

At first sight, this position of Lenin seems theoretically sophisticated (not to speak of its seeming success in 1917) : it takes into account the duality of the subject-object, the notion of the social totality, the idea of the negation of the negation, and the importance of mediations in the struggle for political power. But there are problems, not the least of which was clearly stated in Marx's Third Thesis on Feuerbach: The educator must himself be educated.[26] If the party is the consciousness of the class, either it exists within history, and then it cannot be said to know the course of history for it too is a part and maker of history; or the party is the absolute consciousness, and then we have the problem of a nondialectical subject which theoretically is not possible, and in practice gives rise to the Stalinist state. The dichotomy must, therefore, be relativized; and it is precisely the practical, tactical genius of Lenin to have been able to strike a median path during the events of 1917. But the problem is that theory cannot account, save in terms of common sense, for this median path. Thus, Merleau-Ponty's description of the role of the party strikes one as incredibly sophistical. Several citations will give the reader a taste of this:

Revolutionary action rests on these two principles: that *the party is always right* in the last instance, and that in the last instance *no one is right against the proletariat.*[27]

The party doesn't know everything, doesn't see everything; and yet its authority is absolute because, if spontaneous history has a chance to become manifest history, it can only be in it. . . . In the absence of any metaphysics of history, the dialectic of the proletariat and the party unites in itself and carries all the others: Marxist philosophy has as its final condition not what the proletarians think, not what the party thinks that they should think, but the recognition by the proletariat of its own action in the politics that the party presents it. . . . The party is thus at once everything and nothing: it is nothing but the mirror in which the forces of the proletariat, dispersed throughout the world, concentrate themselves; it is everything because without it, the truth "in itself" would never become manifest, would never complete itself as truth.[28]

It is not a question of letting the proletariat decipher the conjuncture and elaborate the politics and the line. It is not even a question of continually translating in clear terms for the proletariat the revolutionary implications of their actions: that would sometimes make them feel too much the weight of the resistances to be vanquished, resistances that they will surmount without knowing it, and it would in all events alert the adversary. The theoretician thus marches ahead of the proletariat, but only one step ahead as Lenin said; that is, the masses are never the simple means for a grand politics elaborated behind their backs. Led (entraînés) but not manoeuvered, they give the party's politics the seal of its truth.[29]

The party is thus like a mystery of reason: it is the place in history where the *sense that exists* is understood, where the concept comes alive. . . .[30]

What seems to appeal to Merleau-Ponty in this Leninist position is its recognition of the role of contingency in history: sometimes the proletariat is ahead of the party; sometimes the party leads the masses; but always there is a built-in flexibility and interaction whereby theory and practice mediate one another. "The secret of Leninism," he writes, "was in the communication that he managed to establish between the masses and the leaders, between the working class and its 'consciousness.' "[31] In this sense, the Leninist view fits Merleau-Ponty's views.

Merleau-Ponty does see problems in Leninism. One goal of *Adventures of the Dialectic* is to show how this dialectical conception turns against itself, hiding reality under what becomes a fixed schematism. Speaking of Trotsky's hesitation to attack Stalin and to admit that Russia had undergone a Thermidor, he writes that "Trotsky didn't lack the courage to speak a truth that he already knew, nor the combativity to defend it: he hesitated to put the truth outside the party because Marxism had taught him that, on principle, the truth cannot live anywhere but at the junction of the proletariat and the organization which incarnates it." [32] Moreover, this conception of the party easily gave way to the Stalinist dictatorship over the class in the name of the class. In it, the locus of the revolution is decentered away from the proletariat to "its" party; and when the proletariat is not permitted to "decipher the conjuncture and elaborate the politics and the line," or even to have the party's politics translated into clear terms for it, then this "mystery of reason" creates only a passive proletariat which exchanges one ruling class for another without changing the structure of its own life and consciousness.

What is striking is that Merleau-Ponty attributes this theory to Marx. When he recognizes its failure, he argues against Lefort [33] that it is necessary not only to renounce bolshevism but Marxism as well. While it is certainly possible to find statements in Marx which would support the Leninist theory—and, like a good Talmudic scholar, Lenin indeed found most of them—there is one fundamental text which determined the direction of Marx's life's work, and which runs directly counter to the Leninist view: the *Critique of Hegel's Philosophy of the State.*[34] The fundamental lesson of this essay, and of Marxism generally, is that the relation between the spheres of civil society and the state has been inverted by Lenin as well as by Hegel, and that the locus of revolution is not in the political sphere as such but in that of *daily life*. If the revolution is nothing but the capture of state power and its use to restructure the economy—which presupposes, of course, that there is a one-to-one correspondence between the infrastructure and the superstructure and that thus people's lives will be changed, something which Merleau-Ponty and the Western Marxist tradition strongly deny— then perhaps the Leninist view is the correct one: for to a centralized power one can only oppose another centralized power. But, if the revolution is a revolution in daily life, if the revolutionary subject and the revolutionary object are one and the same, then that view of the party has to be rejected. Merleau-Ponty's views on this problem are not unambiguous: he often recognizes the crucial role of the subject, but at the same time more often than not he finds himself concerned with how the party will govern, how it will deal with the contingencies of its circumstances, how it will accomplish the necessary primitive accumulation, etc., etc. This is why he rejects the notion of the permanent revolution and why he polemicizes against Daniel Guérin's insistence on direct democracy and government from the bottom up as "a pompous political concept with which one clothes the Apocalypse. It is the dream of an 'end of politics' which one uses as a political line." [35] However, the point is that direct democracy from the base is not a political concept, save, perhaps, in a derivative sense; it is a social concept, and the revolution of today is a social revolution.

Paradoxically, however, despite his misreading of Marx on this point, Merleau-Ponty's work can be seen as an important contribution to radical thought precisely in the sense that it is concerned with a *social* revolution. In the discussion of Western Marxism, he writes: "It is very superficial to say that Marxism reveals to us the sense of history: it makes us solidary with our time and with its partialities; it does not describe the future, it doesn't make us stop our interrogation but on the contrary deepens it." [36] This is precisely the point! As I suggested at the outset, it is here that we have to look for Merleau-Ponty's contribution to political thought today.

In a significant passage, Merleau-Ponty asserts that it was Hegel "who started the attempt to explore the irrational and integrate it into an expanded reason which remains the task of our century." [37] Hegel's explanation, however, was hindered by his idealist supposition of an end of History where the Spirit would know itself in the world. When Marx stood Hegel on his feet, he did not simply replace the Hegelian Spirit with Matter; what took place was a shift in rationality insofar as Marxian matter is not simply other than the Spirit but rather is dialectical, burdened with the traces of the human subject, opaque and multifaceted like the perceptual object. [38] The task of philosophy then becomes not to "decompose our relationship with the world into real elements, or even into ideal references which would make of it an ideal object, but it discerns articulations in the world, it awakens in it regular relations of pre-possession, of recapitulation, of overlapping, which are as dormant in our ontological landscape, subsist there only in the form of traces, and nevertheless continue to function there, continue to institute the new there." [39] In its historical givenness, the present is "thick," rich with meaning accessible to philosophical interrogation because lived by all. This is why Merleau-Ponty insists, in the preface to *The Phenomenology of Perception,* that "the true philosophy is re-learning to see the world, and in this sense the telling of a story can signify the world with as much 'profundity' as a philosophical treatise." [40] Or, in another essay: "Perhaps there is no news item, however small, which cannot lead to profound thoughts." [41] The foundation of philosophy is the lived world which we share and coconstitute; this insight is common to phenomenology and Marxism. The phenomenologist who writes of Marxism that "one would be tempted to say that it does not base history and modes of thinking on production and the modes of working, but more generally on the mode of existence and co-existence, on interhuman relations," [42] is not falsifying any but a trite interpretation of Marxism. By re-calling to it its foundations, by interrogating it in terms of concrete, not abstract, first principles, the phenomenologist not only makes a contribution to the renewal of Marxism, but shows how the direction of his own interrogation has been shaped by the Marxist problematic.

Merleau-Ponty's critique of Sartre—both of his politics in *Adventures of the Dialectic,* and his ontology in *The Visible and the Invisible*—has its roots in the same notion of an intersubjective world. Sartre's overly rationalistic opposition of the "in itself" and the "for itself," the object and the subject, prevents him from dealing with the concrete present in any but a schematic manner. "The question," writes Merleau-Ponty, "is to know whether as Sartre says there exist only *men* and *things,* or whether there also exists that inter-world [*intermonde*] which we call history, symbolism, truth-to-be-realized." [43] While Sartre's *Critique of Dialectical Reason,* which Merleau-Ponty did not discuss due to his untimely death, goes a long way toward answering this criticism when Sartre introduces the notion of the "practico-inert," it can still be maintained that Merleau-Ponty has struck home.[44]

Merleau-Ponty's service to philosophical reflection is precisely his continual and persistant stress on the "inter-world," with its density and stratifications. Against Marx, he insists that "the Marxism of the young Marx like the Western Marxism of 1923 lacked the means of expressing the inertia of the infrastructures, the resistance of the economic and even the natural conditions, the swallowing up of 'personal relations' in the 'things.' As they described it, history lacked thickness, permitted its sense to appear too soon. It was necessary that they learn the slowness of the mediations." [45] It is within this interworld that the daily lives of humankind are played out; and it is these daily lives which guide and focus the philosophical interrogation. "Metaphysical consciousness has no other objects than those of experience: this world, other people, human history, truth, culture. But instead of taking them as all settled, as consequences with no premises, as if they were self-evident, it rediscovers their fundamental strangeness to me and the miracle of their appearing." [46] Here, philosophy returns to its origins in wonder, and since the philosopher is in the world—as Merleau-Ponty puts it, "After all, the world is all around me, not in front of me" [47]—he wonders not about abstract otherness, but about the facts, large and small, that compose his daily life.

The philosopher's wonder, and his daily life, are situated in the visual and corporeal world which he shares with all; his task is to unveil the structures of that world, the invisible beneath or within the visible. "That is what Marx understood perfectly when he espoused Balzac. . . . Marx wanted to say that a certain manner of *making visible* the world of money and the conflicts of modern society was more important than Balzac's ideas, even his political ones, and that once that vision was acquired it would bring with it its consequences, with or without the Balzac's consent." [48] The task of the artist, like that of the politician, is to lead people to values which they will subsequently recognize as their own.[49] This is the task of the philosopher as well, and it is in this sense that Merleau-Ponty's philosophy can be understood as political.[50]

With Merleau-Ponty, the commentator is tempted to speak of a philosophy of the body politic. The crux of his work, the axis around which it turns, the source and the result of his interrogation is the wonder of human embodiment. The fact that I am not an "I think" but an "I can" comes from my being a thing in the world of things, the flesh of the world and the world of the flesh. It is in terms of my embodiment that I can understand my being-with others in an inter-subjective world which we codetermine and which determines us in return. The fact that "our body is a being with two leaves, on the one hand a thing among things and, on the other, that which sees and touches the things; . . . its belonging both to the order of the 'object' and to that of the 'subject' uncovers for us very unexpected relations between these two orders." [51] One cannot read of this notion of the body as subject-object without recalling Lukács's theory of the proletariat as the subject-object of history. The analogy only holds, however, if my embodiment is considered not as an individual, atomistic incarnation of a cogito in the world, but rather as a collective embodiment. In this sense, the notion of embodiment serves a twofold purpose: on the one hand, it warns against the error of objectivist thought, the thought of a disincarnated, transcendental ego which, by virtue of its intellectualist attempt to disincarnate itself, can only falsify the situation. More important, it accounts for the negative, the incomplete and perspective aspect of the world in which we live. This negativity is important because it is nothing other than the motor of the dialectical movement, that force which drives it onward and which implies that human history is "contingent and . . . the date of the revolution is written on no wall nor in any metaphysical heaven." [52] In that the source of negativity —or "non-sense," as Merleau-Ponty calls it—is human, its elimination or clarification must also have human roots. Moreover, that negativity is not of a political or economic nature alone; it is present in the everyday world by virtue of the very subjective-objective constitution of that world.

From Merleau-Ponty's analysis of the lived world of daily life, of language, art, and history, certain political conclusions follow which would seem to imply that the "sublime point" which he rejected in Marxism because of the problem of the party is not in fact to be so rashly thrown aside. This world is contingent, rife with accident and chance. Yet to speak of this contingency as an objective fact is to violate the notion of the incarnate subject, the basis of Merleau-Ponty's phenomenological dialectic. If the world is contingent, it is so because of the nature of the subject-object, humankind, as well as because of the world of natural things. The world, Merleau-Ponty writes, is a question to which the body replies.[53] It is not, however, an unchanging, pregiven and eternally fixed thing; it is sedimented, overlayed with visible and invisible traces of the human project. Moreover, it is historical, and this is the central dimension.

History is judge. Not History as the Power of a movement or of a century, but history as that bond in which are united, inscribed and accumulated, beyond the limits of centuries or countries, all that we have said and done that is most true and most valid.[54]

What we have here is nothing other than a reformulation of Marx's *Gattungswesen,* interpreted here as the horizon of historical intentionality, and hence that *telos* or end in terms of which we can understand our human progress. This notion of history, rooted in the lived-experience which serves as the ground for all of Merleau-Ponty's interrogations, replaces the mechanistic Communist notion of an end to humanity's development with an openness of possibilities whose exact structure the phenomenological-Marxian analysis of each historical moment would reveal.

There is, however, a problem here which is sharply raised by Henri Lefèbvre's contribution to *The Misadventures of Anti-Marxism.* It can be asserted that "the philosophy of ambiguity justifies [the present] situation instead of denouncing it." [55] Merleau-Ponty himself anticipates this criticism:

Perhaps the reader will say here that we leave him without an answer, and that we limit ourselves to a "So it is" which explains nothing. . . . But when it is a question of speaking [*la parole*] or of the body or of history, unless one wants to destroy what one seeks to understand . . . one can only show the paradox of the expression.[56]

When, in *The Visible and the Invisible,* Merleau-Ponty speaks of the earth as the Ur-Arche, the carnal prehistory; when he talks of the need for a transcendental geology, and of the importance of geography, is one not tempted to see a passive acceptance of a pregiven destiny? [57] Or, when he defines his conception of the role of the philosopher today:

Efficacious or not, it is to clarify the ideological situation, to underline beyond the paradoxes and the contingencies of present history the true terms of the human problem, to recall to the Marxists their humanist inspiration, to recall to the democracies their fundamental hypocrisy, and to maintain intact against all propaganda the chances that history might once again become clear.[58]

There is unquestionably a tendency toward an ontologization of the present social problems which occludes their immediate call for a resolution, a call echoed in the voices of the masses from the Third World to the migrant workers of France and America. When Merleau-Ponty writes that "political problems have their source in the fact that we are all subjects and that, nonetheless, we see and treat the Other as object," [59] it is easy to caricature this as philosophical obscurantism.[60] This same criticism can be prolonged by a discussion of Merleau-Ponty's theory of painting, which affirms that each painter renews from the beginning the same task of opening up the visual world.

Such interpretations are not to be wished away. The central problem raised by Merleau-Ponty concerns the *telos*, the directionality, sense and rationality of political action. What does it mean to pretend to offer the world new directions, radical social change, a new political existence? With what justification can we pretend to raise the banner of revolution? How are we to escape the dilemmas of past revolutions? What is the ground of our truth-claims? The notion of the incarnate consciousness as an "I can" situated in a human-natural world whose analysis is its own psychoanalysis, and whose psychoanalysis is the analysis of the world, provides a direction for further interrogation.

8
Ronald Bruzina

MERLEAU-PONTY AND HUSSERL
THE IDEA OF SCIENCE

THE MODERN classic philosopher is one who conceives philosophy as radical self-understanding. For him reflective inquiry probes ultimately into the nature and grounds of reflective inquiry itself and reaches thereby that level which endows the philosophic enterprise with its fundamental legitimacy and radicality. Husserl and Merleau-Ponty are of this mind, and the subject of this essay as their convergence and divergence as their thought attempts to think this ultimate question of reason's self-understanding.

Casting the question into the form in which Husserl conceives it provides a sharp focus on the central issue. Husserl sees the question of rationality quite simply as the question of science *(scientia)*. For him philosophy is constituted by the idea of science, so that the tradition of philosophy *is* the tradition of science. The history of Western intellectual life is therefore the history at once of Western philosophy and Western science. Now it is not this entire thesis that will be considered, but only one of its elements; and that is simply the idea of science—as *idea,* on the one hand, and as *science* on the other. Given the limits of space, I have chosen to concentrate on two texts of equivalent station with regard to the corpus of the work of the two men, texts, that is, of final (and unfinished) interpretative reassumption and reconsideration. These texts are for Husserl, *The Crisis* papers,[1] and for Merleau-Ponty, *The Visible and the Invisible.*[2] Consideration of the main theme out of these texts comprises two levels: 1) the idea of science as to what it affirms and ordains or prescribes; and 2) the question of inquiring into this idea itself, i.e., the question of the exercise of the idea reflecting back upon itself.

The twenty-five years that separate Husserl's essay on philosophy in the first volume of *Logos* in 1911 [3] and his lectures on the renewal of European rationality given in Vienna and Prague in 1935 [4] mark a difference in worlds. In 1911 confidence in human progress through rigorous scientific study was typified in the very founding of *Logos*. Husserl's contribution to the journal, though proposing a more rigorously and radically self-critical vision of science, asserted nevertheless a like primacy for rational and theoretical modes of thought. In principle, submitting the universe to rational inquiry was a common affirmation. But in 1935, after a murderous world war and with the spiraling emergence of fascist and racist national-ism around him, even in the universities, together with what to Husserl was the exaggeration of existential concerns into sheer irrationalism, there seemed no longer to be any such common faith. In 1911 Husserl's antagonists were scientific naturalism and histori-cal relativism which nonetheless asserted themselves as strictly ra-tional theories. In 1935 rationality as such seemed at the point of being dismissed. *The Crisis* lectures, then, offer a defense of reason itself, for which Husserl's now mature phenomenology was to serve as the instrument for radical self-understanding.

The opening sections of *The Crisis* comprising part 1 make this quite clear. Yet Husserl makes equally clear that a defense of reason is not simply an affirmation of modern empirical science. For some-one to identify rational inquiry with positivistic science is to narrow the idea which lies at the origin of the inquiry called scientific. Only when theoretical inquiry is maintained in its total scope and validity does it remain what was originally born as *philosophia*. That is to say, the idea of science as "the one all-encompassing science, the science of the totality of what is" [5] is identical with the idea of phi-losophy; and this indentification is repeatedly emphasized in *The Crisis*.

The idea of science is considerably broader than the modern understanding of *science*, defined more or less as fact-gathering and fact-organization under the ordering guidance of a hypothetical, inference-rich formal systematic. There is a fundamental difference to be made explicit, a difference not in the ultimate operative thrust but in the awareness of that ultimate constitution and motivation and therefore a difference in the conception of the concrete scope, form, and direction inquiry is to take. The difference lies in this, that science in the true and full sense consciously articulates itself as *reason;* and we will get to this shortly. At the moment we must note that for Husserl the reduction of the idea of science to its modern understanding incapacitates that idea, making it unable ultimately to assert itself as reason against an insurgence of skepticism and irrationalism.[6] If science is only science in the modern experimental sense, its procedures preclude the theoretical explication and critical valuation of *episteme* as such against *doxa,* of the knowledge of what *is* against the acceptance of what is naïvely only thought to be—which is a distinction foundational to the very idea of rational inquiry.

What is required, then, is a type of inquiry which both embodies and inquires into the idea of science which Husserl sees as generating and grounding the Western intellect. Reassumption and critical, radical self-understanding have to take place in order for science to be science and thereby for philosophy to *be.*[7] If such a project can be genuinely undertaken, then philosophy will exist as scientific in a true sense and science will be theoretically validated as genuine, rational knowledge.

Husserl's historical reflections in *The Crisis* deal mainly with the modern period. How science and philosophy are transformed by the Galilean enterprise and the Cartesian effort is the main theme of large portions of the work. It is in the historical situation of inheritance of this transformation that Husserl's own philosophy takes up its task. Nevertheless, while analyzing the process of transmission and exploitation of this inheritance through Hume and Kant into contemporary thought, Husserl constantly recalls the elements that persist even while being transformed, that is, the elements that constitute the Western idea of rational inquiry, the elements that have their origin in the Greek "primal establishment." There is, then, a double focus: 1) the institution of philosophy in the Greek experience, and 2) the transformation of this into a new project at the beginning of the modern era. For Husserl these two moments together are responsible for the project of rationality which characterizes the modern period, although the critical understanding of their essentials is lacking.

Now the points I wish to draw from Husserl's exposition of the idea of science are simple, possibly banal, but absolutely irreducible and fundamental. Summarily put, they are as follows:

1) Seeking reasons constitutes rational inquiry.

2) Reasons are sought for what *is* in terms of what *is*.

3) What is and reasons for it, as sought by inquiring consciousness, are made ideals for thought; and rational inquiry is an endless effort to achieve the ideal in actual, concrete knowledge.

The first two of these points are usually taken as self-evident. However, these are precisely matters requiring reflection, i.e., demanding inquiry into the origin and grounding of their sense. The third point is the one that requires the more careful consideration here, for the greatest misunderstanding of Husserl's aim for philosophy as science (scientia) occurs with regard to this matter of the ideal and the eidetic. We shall take these points one by one.

"Philosophy . . . is essentially a science of true beginnings, or origins, of *rizomata panton*." [8] Any text of Husserl's follows this thesis. Philosophy is reason seeking true and basic reasons. *The Crisis* repeats the same idea even more emphatically. The opening paragraph of part 3B, sec. 56, Husserl's recapitulation of his analyses up to that point, fairly bristles with statements of this kind, of which just one can serve as a typical example:

. . . the style of a truly scientific transcendental philosophy—"truly scientific" in the sense that it works up from the bottom in self-evident single steps and is thus in truth ultimately grounded and ultimately grounding. We attempted thereby to awaken the full insight that only such a philosophy, through such a regressive inquiry back to the last conceivable ground in the transcendental ego, can fulfill the meaning which is inborn in philosophy from its primal establishment.[9]

Rationality, then, both in its Greek origin and in its modern transformation, is the articulate inquiry after grounds and sources, and this thrust is constitutive of philosophy/science, of science. The specification of particular types of reasons, grounds, or origins would spell a differentiation of disciplines, of "sciences." Yet philosophy or science as such is *one* in this respect, that it necessarily seeks reasons of some sort in some way.

This is not all there is, however. Nonscientific consciousness also seeks the causes of occurrences. What differentiates scientific inquiry from nonscientific is the kind of value-ascription with which the reason to be sought is endowed. Prescientific inquiry is satisfied with reasons proportionate to practical needs and interests. Particularity and approximation are not defects; they suit the practical typicality of everyday concrete world experience. But the scientific spirit—still taking *scientific* in its more comprehensive sense—seeks reasons that have the character of what is always and everywhere for anyone, of what is "a norm for all knowledge." [10] The very distinction: *episteme/doxa,* is the distinction between the comprehension of what is in itself and the acceptance of what merely seems to be as determined by particular circumstances. "Philosophy in its ancient origins wanted to be 'science,' universal knowledge of the universe of what is; it wanted to be not vague and relative everyday knowledge—δόξα—but rational knowledge—ἐπιστήμη." [11] Absolute universality, independence from circumstantial particularization (change, viewpoint, contingency), is the property of being as rational inquiry aims to know it. This kind of knowing, *episteme,* is rationality in its highest exercise, and Husserl's way of speaking of the two together makes this unmistakable.

Now a problem arises, and it is Husserl who spells it out in *The Crisis.* [12] Can I or anyone, as a concrete human conscious subject, ever achieve this kind of absolute grasp of anything? Is this aim, posed for rationality, achievable by some concrete rational mind? Human experience, even when conceived as corrected either by one's own continued inquiry or by exchange with others, is always relative, "and thus all descriptive assertions are necessarily relative, and all conceivable inferences, deductive or inductive, are relative. How can thinking achieve anything but relative truths? . . . Is this [idea of 'truth in itself'] together with its correlate, what exists in itself, not a philosophical invention?" [13] No, Husserl answers himself, it is not a fiction. It is the very institution of a new level of human life, the level precisely of activity following the ideal of scientific thinking. Now, the key notion in understanding this new level is the familiar distinction, now fully drawn out, between the ideal, and the actual and concrete.

Let us first distinguish two orders for *idea* itself; that of the total project of the mind which is the idea of rationality, the idea of philosophy, the idea of science; and that of any particular theme of inquiry in philosophy or science, such as the idea of soul, of intention, of irrational number, of quantum, etc. Consider the second sense of *idea* first. With regard to some phenomenon or group of phenomena, rational inquiry seeks comprehension in terms of what is by disclosing reasons. The phenomenon has some sense already for the inquirer—the situation which Husserl in *The Crisis* precisely wishes to expose through his notion of the life-world—but this sense is imprecise and variable. Inquiry as rational aims to find something of the given sense-manifold that is unvarying and set, as well as generally true of all similar phenomena. Intelligible accounting proposes uncovering of the essentials of something, by considering it on the one hand as a discriminable item in itself—*what* it is —and on the other by taking it back to the reasons (grounds, origins, etc.) for it, themselves in terms of their essentials. Put in Husserlian terminology, rational inquiry is constitutionally eidetic. To seek to know rationally is to seek to know eidetically. The *idea* of something is that of it which is to be known as to its essential structure.

This means, then, that the idea of a "truth in itself" is not a fiction but the very correlate of the aim to know with scientific justification. At the same time the idea of "truth in itself" is precisely an idea, while the aim to know with *episteme*/science, in contrast to *doxa,* is itself equally an ideal project. That is to say, it is the posing of a value ascription on an absolute order as the aim of an action only possible on a relative order. Yet, the posing of this absolute order as ideal is precisely what institutes the concrete action in question, namely, inquiry into true reasons for the true being of things. To seek the true idea of something is to put into an action a project in strict accord with the exigencies of the idea of science.

What is crucial now is to follow Husserl in the way he draws out the implications of this: "True being is *everywhere* an ideal goal, a task of *episteme* or 'reason,' as opposed to being which through *doxa* is merely thought to be, unquestioned and 'obvious'." [14] He goes on to explain that even in the ultimate form of this task, namely as intersubjective and communal, the project of reason is an endless one, necessitating a ceaseless progression of only relative accomplishments: ". . . rationality is an idea residing in the infinite and is *de facto* necessarily [only] on the way." [15] Rationality, the idea of science, the institution of a teleological project for mankind as such had begun with the Greeks and was transmuted at the beginning of the modern period. Immense implications for considerations of culture set aside, the point to be emphasized here is precisely this teleological character of science as an unachievable yet endlessly renewed effort to gain actually in knowledge what is posed ideally as the truth of something, to gain concretely what is ideal as to both the absoluteness of a grasp and the absoluteness of what is grasped.

What Husserl does here is to lay the basis for uncovering confusions that characterize much of the commentary on his phenomenology, particularly as to his concentration on the order of ideality, the conditions for genuine knowledge, and the moment of the transcendental, especially when this commentary involves a socially oriented critique of scientism. Out of Husserl's analyses we learn the utmost necessity for distinguishing between the moment of reason and the movements of reasoning minds. Failure to recognize this distinction shows in confusions such as that between the theoretical idea of the primary value of action in human life, together with the theoretical assertion of facticity in the conditions of human inquiry (interest, value bias, etc.), on the one hand, and on the other the blindness of a particular theorizing agent in not recognizing the value, assumptions, and interest orientations of his personal inquiry, and therefore in not recognizing his essential falling short of the ideal of true science. The point is that thinking, which shows these confusions, has simply not reached a clear understanding of what is implied by the very rationality of the critique or inquiry it undertakes, whereas Husserl is constantly concerned with clearly probing the sense of what "clearly probing the sense of" means, i.e., his aim is ultimate self-consciousness for reason. "Thus philosophy is nothing other than . . . ratio in the constant movement of self-elucidation, begun with the first breakthrough of philosophy into mankind, whose innate reason was previously in a state of concealment, of nocturnal obscurity." This is quite simply ultimate science grounding all other scientific efforts.

One final point remains, one implicit in the section just completed, but needing explicit statement. Rational inquiry, being eidetic, aims at actual complete knowledge of what is posed ideally as the idea of something. For example, with regard to the most widely adapted topic of *The Crisis* studies, the *Lebenswelt*, Husserl says: "the life-world does have, in all its relative features, a *general structure*. This general structure, to which everything that exists relatively is bound, is not itself relative. We can attend to it in its generality and, with sufficient care, fix it once and for all in a way equally accessible to all." [16] Eidetic inquiry, i.e., any rational inquiry, precisely in undertaking inquiry into some topic, *poses* that topic as the theme of inquiry. This thematization, as the posing of the theme, is not a substitution of some fiction for reality. It is the posing of a really experienced significance as "what-is-to-be-known." However, unlike everyday, nonscientific questioning, here the theme is posed as "what-is-to-be-known-with-the-value: what-*is*," i.e., with the value "true unconditionally." In other words, when a significance is inquired into theoretically, that is, rationally, scientifically, philosophically, it is posed as *idea*. In Husserlian terms, when a significance is inquired into in theoretical reason, it is constituted as the ideal correlate of a specified noetic intentional effort.

Here we would rejoin the results of Husserl's earlier writing in phenomenology. There is, however, no room for showing the connection with principal themes in *Logical Investigations* or *Ideas*, or *Formal and Transcendental Logic*, for example, and I can only allude to a basic consistency and unity in Husserl's phenomenology on the point of the constitution of ideality and the conditions for scientific knowledge.[17] We have what is sufficient, nevertheless, to read Merleau-Ponty now on the question of the idea of philosophy as science.

It is quite possible to find a continuity of theme in the thought of Merleau-Ponty arching from *Phenomenology of Perception* to the latest, posthumously collected and published, of his personal researches. One could in particular make a fairly neat concordance on the theme of a critique of the idea of the pure and absolute subject. Between the cogito of *Phenomenology of Perception* and "Reflection and Interrogation" and "Interrogatation and Intuition" in *The Visible and the Invisible* clear similarities can easily be found.

Such a study could have the merit of offering a systematic for clarifying a Merleau-Pontian phenomenology, yet, apart from its value as introductory, it would have two faults: it would make a doctrinal system out of what was essentially a dialectical inquiry, and it would suggest a rigidly limited focus for Merleau-Ponty's thought, namely, the Cartesian ontological schema. Now it may well be true that Merleau-Ponty conducts his critique of consciousness too narrowly by taking the idealist option of the Cartesian split, the "pure spectator" who creates all sense in his cognized world, as the necessary paradigm for any philosophy that insists that reflection is the mode of rational knowing. *Reflective philosophy* becomes accordingly synonymous with belief in what for Merleau-Ponty is an impossible state for human consciousness, namely, as absolute constitutive surveyor of the scene of sense. We find this as strong a train of argument in *The Visible and the Invisible* as in *Phenomenology of Perception,* in the chapters just mentioned for example, despite their twenty-odd years of difference in age.

Now the details of this argument are not the topic here, but rather some elements involved in the very conducting of it. Merleau-Ponty offers serious criticisms against various views of the nature of consciousness inspired at least in part by an appreciation of conditions imposed by the aim of cognitive grasp of truth. Yet, while offering criticism, Merleau-Ponty remarks that he in no wise intends to disqualify reflection "in favor of the unreflected (which we know only through reflection). It is a question not of putting perceptual faith in place of reflection, but on the contrary of taking into account the total situation, which involves reference from the one to the other." [18] Not the rejection of reflection but of an absolutized view of it is his aim, a view such as one that makes it an absolute source of meaning or limits its efficacy to a supposed other-worldly vision of essences, which for Merleau-Ponty amounts to the same mistake. His aim is to uncover the character of consciousness in general as not an absolute of this kind or any other, but rather as something intimately participant in the thrust of bodily intentionality which is human being-in-a-world. Merleau-Ponty aims at bringing to light the nonreflective conditions prior to reflection in which, nonetheless, sense is made of things in a dynamic way: "this non-knowing of the beginning which is not nothing, and which is not reflective truth either, and which also must be accounted for." [19]

Now the problem is this: what kind of reflection is Merleau-Ponty's *own* if it is not itself to imply any absolute relationship of the grasp of truth to its subject matter, which is at the source of the philosophic views of consciousness he criticizes? He clearly intends his own reflection to function in such a way as to rectify these other views of reflection while not imposing a rival metaphysics of consciousness of equal absoluteness. Is this possible? Understanding consciousness (and therefore understanding understanding) for Merleau-Ponty is a matter of finding an adequate way of conceiving the duality of involvement and detachment that constitutes the possibility of knowing. He sees this ambivalent condition in the fact of human consciousness being bodily. In the condition of being bodily, Merleau-Ponty suggests, "the presence of the world is precisely the presence of its flesh to my flesh." [20] Moreover, "that I 'am of the world' and that I am not it," as the condition of there being a "distance which does not prevent us from knowing it, which is on the contrary the guarantee for knowing it," all this is forgotten by philosophies of consciousness. Husserl, however, did not overlook it. On the contrary, he performed the analyses that uncovered it, and Merleau-Ponty acknowledges his debt (at least indirectly). [21] But while Merleau-Ponty now wishes to articulate as fully as possible this structure of involvement and dynamism in the "flesh" of being that generates both perceptual sense-filled experience and the movement to reflective sense-probing—which is the real subject of *The Visible and the Invisible* [22]—he refuses one idea of Husserl's as invalid in his own inquiry, a notion absolutely fundamental to Husserl's phenomenology and therefore pivotal in any relationship between the thought of the two men.

This notion is the idea that cognitive consciousness in its primary general form is a posing consciousness, that consciousness acts to set up what is to be sense for it, that any sense for conciousness is a noematic/objective theme for itself as noetic/subjective agent.[23] Such a notion of consciousness is for Merlau-Ponty what taints the correlative notion of essence, essence being accordingly that universal representation that displays the true sense of any reality in an absolute and pure way, unmixed with ambiguity, contingency, and uncertainty. Concrete being, i.e., the sense that consciousness has its life in the world, Merleau-Ponty points out, is in no way like such "essences," just as actual consciousness-in-the-world is in no way like the pure spectator required of this kind of "essence."

Merleau-Ponty's reproach is, in effect, that Husserl tends to see consciousness as cognitive necessarily in terms of the constituting subject for whom and by whom the object is posed in an explicit thematizing action.[24] And he asks: if consciousness is like this, how will it ever be possible for it to know the structure of its own origin since this structure does not share the conditions required for this kind of thematic posing? In reply, however, one has to reproach Merleau-Ponty with an opposite tendency, namely, to describe consciousness as if it in no way really poses objects in thematic consideration, as if the only genuine intentionality were that of the operative flux of temporal development and sedimentation, while any thematic intentionality that goes out toward an identity of meaning as toward an object is false or radically falsifying. Yet is not Merleau-Ponty's argument an instance of precisely this kind of posing of a theme as an idea to be gained in as adequate a cognition as possible?

Now this debate can be approached from two directions: 1) from the point of view of philosophic thinking considered as the science begun with the Greeks, and 2) from the point of view of a questioning of that very concept of philosophy as science with the implication thereby that philosophy holds secret within itself a dimension of articulate revelation that is other than scientific theoretical analysis.

Now it may well be that Husserl does construct his phenomenology on the basis of an interpretation of cognitive consciousness in terms primarily of subject-object act-intentionality. Nevertheless the question remains whether his principle is correct for at least a certain dimension of consciousness, even if it does not hold for all consciousness. The point of this paper is to view Merleau-Ponty's reflections on philosophy within the perspective of Husserl's analysis of consciousness on the point of the idea of science. If we take Merleau-Ponty's reflections as sharing the goal of rational, articulate exposition of the general structure of the phenomenon of human consciousness, then the following points must be made.

Merleau-Ponty may reject a certain position regarding the structure of consciousness (the empiricist, idealist, or intuitionist), but he need not and indeed cannot reject the idea of science as *idea*. That is, the ideally posed acquisition of absolute, circumstance-independent truth may be the aim of reflection without the actual operative structure of consciousness being concretely indentifiable exclusively as characterized in fact by the ideal conditions of such acquisition. The whole or even the ground level of consciousness need not be subject-object thematization in order for some dimension of it to be precisely that, especially if this dimension itself is not a pure subjective act, instant, total, maximally efficacious. Nevertheless, the idea of this kind of pure subject-object acquisition can remain as motivating exemplar for a certain type of knowing which is never fully achieved and yet does possess a subject-object thematization polarity as one dimension of its reality.

Now Merleau-Ponty's argument is a forceful critique precisely of the mistaken identification of the *pure idea* of rational knowing with the *real phenomenon* of consciousness in its concrete life, along with the distorted view of human being that results. But he performs this critique without himself spelling out an appreciation of that idea as idea, i.e., science as ideal *telos* for the project of rational inquiry, in the way Husserl does. As a consequence, Merleau-Ponty's critique may seem to be a rejection of the very idea of science. (On another level, his critique *is* directed at the idea of science, but from below.) Nevertheless, Merleau-Ponty's reflections, at least on one level, are a continual progression under the impetus of that very idea, in a thematization-consciousness of certain topics. The themes he poses are precisely ideas to be investigated for their truth beyond the insufficiencies and distortions of previous philosophies. Indeed, in an earlier text, "Phenomenology and the Sciences of

Man," [25] (although not in *The Visible and the Invisible*), he explicitly espouses an Husserlian understanding of philosophy as idea and of consciousness as thematizing, quoting Husserl's own words from his Afterword to the *Ideas*.[26] Moreover, that thematization be intentionally constitutive of the eidetic is also acknowledged in these same Sorbonne lectures.[27]

The fact remains, however, that these last references are not part of *The Visible and the Invisible* and do not perhaps reflect the awareness of a question that is precisely a motive for the studies that compose it. What we have said so far can be taken as a corrective or amplification of Merleau-Ponty's thought at a certain level, but one that does not yet reach the ultimate problematic activated in *The Visible and the Invisible*.

Suppose we take Merleau-Ponty's criticisms more directly, assume his objections, and take his reflections as far as they will go. a) Let us begin with a summary of certain points from the text in question; The eidetic form of knowledge, granted its indispensability for rational, scientific knowing (which Merleau-Ponty will admit),[28] can nevertheless never represent accurately the operative, ambivalent flux characteristic of the originating ground of that form of knowledge. Eidetic knowledge is a form of consciousness (thematic, object-intentional) that imposes categorical disjunctions and divisions not found so strictly in actual living experience in a world. Moreover eidetic knowledge fixes in retrospect, while experience flows in anticipation. Eidetic knowledge gains its end by asserting limits and closure; experience lives by renewing and opening. b) Reintroducing the question of Merleau-Ponty's own reflections, we have to conclude that his assertions are not instances of eidetic grasp; otherwise they reestablish implicitly the idea being criticized, the idea of philosophy as eidetic science. They must be taken rather as attempts to clear the ground therapeutically for a radically new procedure for philosophic thought, a truly "other point of departure." [29] In other words, what Merleau-Ponty offers is eidetic reflection following (necessarily) the idea of science but now in the service of a "hyperreflection," a reflection that is not one according to that idea of eidetic rationality. "The legitimate function of the fixing of the eidetic invariants would be no longer to confine us within the consideration of the *what*, but to make evident the divergence between the eidetic invariants and the effective functioning and to invite us to bring the experience itself forth from its obstinate silence. . . ." [30] What is needed is a language in philosophy operating as something "that possesses the signification less than it is possessed by it, that does not speak *of it*, but speaks *it*, or speaks *according to it*, or lets it speak and be spoken within me, breaks through my present." [31]

From this perspective, Merleau-Ponty is seen as trying to activate a type of philosophic consciousness that, while wishing to get beyond subject-object eidetic science, is not advocating either mute contemplativeness nor some kind of immediate fusion with reality. The first would be inarticulate, and the second would eliminate precisely what is required for questioning and understanding, namely, the distance that makes nearness possible.[32] He is aiming for something articulately positive yet revelatory of being in a way other than by scientific exposition.[33]

This, of course, is a far from satisfactory announcement, nor do I wish to try fleshing out what it merely gives notice of. I must leave the matter as Merleau-Ponty has left it, for this is as far as he gets. What I have done at least is to point out this level of thinking in Merleau-Ponty—philosophy as non-science as a counterweight to the theme of philosophy as science obtained from Husserl. For this purpose, however, the matter can be advanced one more step, in a concluding consideration.

In *The Crisis* Husserl wishes his analyses to uncover the ground for that level of consciousness called "scientific reason" in the structure of the life-world. In *The Visible and the Invisible* Merleau-Ponty asserts that reflective analysis is in principle incapable of coming to terms adequately with the ground for scientific rationality. If Merleau-Ponty is correct, then rationality is shown to be incapable of demonstrating its own origin and basis! (And the philosophy he is advocating would presumably be no renewed attempt to do so.) The idea of science is a universe closed in upon itself, unable by reason of its very exigencies and criteria to uncover its own beginnings and justification! Ludwig Landgrebe, in a brilliant article on Husserl's *Erste Philosophie*,[34] argues much to the same effect. For Landgrebe, Husserl is unable adequately to account, in terms of eidetic necessities, for the institution of the project of ultimate rational analysis and justification. He cannot do so because it is Husserl himself who precisely uncovers the historical contingency of that institution, in view particularly of the teleological ideality of the project. For this reason Husserl's phenomenology cannot succeed as the philosophic grounding of philosophy, and therefore of science.

The two critiques, Merleau-Ponty's and Landgrebe's, if taken together, suggest a whole approach to the reading of phenomenology which draws quite close to Heidegger's path of thinking. At the same time it sharpens one's vision for catching the occasional sentence of Husserl's that offers a meaning of striking ambivalence, at once in harmony and at odds with the apparent solid rationality of his work. One such instance is a fitting note on which to end. It occurs in the recapitulation text that Biemel adds to the main text of *The Crisis* as its terminal number. Husserl repeats his aim to offer final self-understanding on the part of reason, giving thereby final understanding on the part of reason, giving thereby final understanding of human being—and then he has this expression of what that means: "mankind understanding itself as rational, understanding that it is rational in seeking to be rational (daß sie vernunftig ist im Vernunftigseinwollen) . . ." [35] In the end, then, is the answer this, that man is rational because he has willed to be?

Notes / Index

NOTES

Preface

1. Maurice Merleau-Ponty, *The Structure of Behavior*, trans. Alden L. Fisher (Boston: Beacon Press, 1963).

2. Maurice Merleau-Ponty, *The Visible and the Invisible*, trans. Alphonso Lingis (Evanston, Ill.: Northwestern University Press, 1968).

3. Claude Levi-Strauss, *The Raw and the Cooked*, trans. John and Doreen Weightman (New York: Harper and Row, 1970), p. 4.

4. Maurice Merleau-Ponty, *Phenomenology of Perception*, trans. Colin Smith (New York: Humanities Press, 1962).

5. Maurice Merleau-Ponty, *Humanism and Terror*, trans. John O'Neill (Boston: Beacon Press, 1969).

6. Maurice Merleau-Ponty, *Sense and Non-Sense*, trans. Hubert L. Dreyfus and Patricia A. Dreyfus (Evanston, Ill.: Northwestern University Press, 1964).

7. Maurice Merleau-Ponty, *Les aventures de la dialectique* (Paris: Gallimard, 1955).

8. Maurice Merleau-Ponty, *Signs*, trans. Richard C. McCleary (Evanston, Ill.: Northwestern University Press, 1964).

9. Maurice Merleau-Ponty, *The Primacy of Perception and Other Essays*, ed. James M. Edie (Evanston, Ill.: Northwestern University Press, 1964), pp. 159–90.

1   In the Folds of the Flesh

1. Maurice Merleau-Ponty, *The Structure of Behavior*, trans. Alden L. Fisher (Boston: Beacon Press, 1963), p. 199.

2. Ibid., p. 166.

3. Ibid., p. 199.

4. Ibid.

5. Ibid., 121.

6. Ibid., pp. 210–11.

7. Ibid., p. 219.

8. Ibid., p. 199.

9. Ibid.

10. Ibid., p. 285 n 82.

11. Ibid., p. 219.

12. Maurice Merleau-Ponty, *Phenomenology of Perception,* trans. Colin Smith (New York: Humanities Press, 1962), p. ix.

13. Ibid., p. xix.

14. Ibid., p. xx.

15. Ibid., p. 57; "Our task will be, moreover, to rediscover phenomena, the layer of living experience through which people and things are first given to us, the system 'Self-others-things' as it comes into being. . . ."

16. Maurice Merleau-Ponty, "An Unpublished Text," trans. Arleen B. Dallery, *The Primacy of Perception,* ed. James M. Edie (Evanston, Ill.: Northwestern University Press, 1964), pp. 3–11.

17. Ibid., p. 5, for the reference to archeology.

18. Ibid., p. 7.

19. Ibid., p. 10.

20. Maurice Merleau-Ponty, *In Praise of Philosophy,* trans. John Wild and James M. Edie (Evanston, Ill.: Northwestern University Press, 1963).

21. Ibid., p. 17.

22. Ibid., p. 19. Translation altered.

23. Ibid., pp. 31–32.

24. Ibid., p. 33.

25. Ibid., p. 36.

26. Ibid., p. 41.

27. Ibid., p. 43.

28. Ibid., p. 44.

29. Ibid., p. 45.

30. Ibid., pp. 58–61.

31. Maurice Merleau-Ponty, *Sense and Non-Sense,* trans. Hubert L. Dreyfus and Patricia A. Dreyfus (Evanston, Ill.: Northwestern University Press, 1964), p. 133.

32. Ibid.

33. Maurice Merleau-Ponty, *The Visible and the Invisible,* trans. Alphonso Lingis (Evanston, Ill.: Northwestern University Press, 1968), p. 174.

34. Ibid., p. 167.

35. Ibid., p. 183.

36. Ibid., p. 186.

37. Ibid.

38. Ibid., p. 187.
39. Ibid., p. 179.
40. Ibid., p. 258.
41. Ibid., p. 259.
42. Ibid., p. 266.
43. Ibid., p. 204.
44. Ibid., pp. 128–29.
45. Ibid., p. 100.
46. Ibid., p. 102.
47. Ibid.
48. Ibid., p. 103.
49. Ibid., p. 39.
50. Ibid., pp. 126–27.
51. Ibid., p. 115.
52. *Phenomenology of Perception,* p. 203 *n* 1.
53. Ibid., p. 221.
54. Ibid., pp. 190–91.
55. Ibid., p. 146.
56. Ibid.
57. Ibid., p. 205.
58. Ibid.
59. Ibid., p. 212.
60. Ibid., p. 214. Translation altered.
61. Ibid. Translation altered.
62. Ibid.
63. Ibid., p. 215. Translation altered.
64. Ibid., p. 217.
65. Ibid., p. 235. Translation altered.
66. Ibid., pp. 326–27.
67. Ibid., 297.
68. "In the introduction (fundamental thought) say that I must show that what one might consider to be 'psychology' (*Phenomenology of Perception*) is in fact ontology"; *The Visible and the Invisible,* "February, 1959," p. 176.
69. *The Structure of Behavior,* pp. 167, 216, and 219.
70. *Phenomenology of Perception,* p. 57.
71. *The Structure of Behavior,* p. 210.
72. Ibid., p. 174.
73. Ibid., p. 167.
74. *Phenomenology of Perception,* pp. 182 and 191.
75. Ibid., p. 183. Translation altered.
76. Ibid., p. 180. Translation altered.
77. Ibid., pp. 183–84.
78. Ibid., pp. 186 and 194.

79. Ibid., p.   166. Translation altered.
80. Ibid., p. 182.
81. Ibid., p. 187.
82. Ibid., p. 188.
83. Ibid., p. 194.
84. Ibid., p. 197. Translation altered.
85. Ibid., p. 394.
86. Ibid., p. 197.
87. Ibid., p. 235.
88. Ibid., p. 186.
89. Ibid., p. 197. Translation altered. For a later statement on the anonymous corporeity of language, see *La prose du monde* (Paris: Gallimard, 1969), pp. 194–95.
90. Ibid., p. 179. Translation altered. See also Maurice Merleau-Ponty, *Signs,* trans. Richard C. McCleary (Evanston, Ill.: Northwestern University Press, 1964), p. 93.
91. Jacques Derrida, *Le voix et le phénomène* (Paris: Presses Universitaires de France, 1967).
92. Edmund Husserl, *Logical Investigations, Volume I,* trans. J. N. Findlay (New York: Humanities Press, 1970), pp. 280–81; Investigation I, "Expression and Meaning," sec. 1–9.
93. *Phenomenology of Perception,* p. 196.
94. *The Visible and the Invisible,* p. 175.
95. Ibid.
96. Ibid., p. 176.
97. *Phenomenology of Perception,* p. 402.
98. Ibid., p. 403.
99. Ibid., p. 404.
100. *Sense and Non-Sense,* p. 88.
101. Ibid., p. 87.
102. "La conscience et l'acquisition du langage," *Maurice Merleau-Ponty à la Sorbonne, Bulletin de Psychologie,* no. 236, 18, 3–6 (November 1964), 257. For Saussure see: Ferdinand de Saussure, *Course in General Linguistics,* ed. Charles Bally and Albert Sechehaye, trans. Wade Baskin (New York: McGraw-Hill, 1966).
103. "La conscience et l'acquisition du langage," p. 257.
104. Ibid., p. 259.
105. Ibid.
106. *La prose du monde,* p. 34.
107. "On the Phenomenology of Language," *Signs,* pp. 86–89.
108. Ibid., p. 91.
109. "Indirect Language and the Voices of Silence," *Signs,* p. 41.
110. Ibid., p. 44.

111. Ibid., p. 73.
112. Ibid., p. 83.
113. Ibid., p. 17.
114. Ibid., p. 18.
115. Ibid., p. 19.
116. Ibid. Translation altered.
117. *The Visible and the Invisible,* pp. 181–82; a "savage mind," p. 175.
118. Ibid., pp. 170–71.
119. Ibid., p. 201.
120. Ibid., p. 29.
121. Ibid., p. 118.
122. Ibid., p. 126.
123. Ibid., p. 119.
124. Ibid., p. 126.
125. Ibid., p. 136.
126. Ibid., p. 148.
127. Ibid., p. 150.
128. Ibid., p. 154.
129. Ibid., p. 151.
130. Ibid., p. 102.

2 Singing the World

1. Maurice Merleau-Ponty, *Phenomenology of Perception,* trans. Colin Smith (London: Routledge and Kegan Paul, 1962) p. 179.
2. Ibid., p. 193.
3. Maurice Merleau-Ponty, "The Primacy of Perception," trans. James M. Edie, *Existential Phenomenology* (London: Prentice-Hall, 1967) p. 41.
4. *Phenomenology of Perception,* p. 177.
5. Ibid., p. 179.
6. Ibid., p. vii.
7. Ibid., p. xiv.
8. Ibid., pp. 178–79.
9. Ibid., p. 179.
10. Ibid., p. 178.
11. Ibid., p. 177.
12. Ibid., p. 177–78.
13. Ibid., p. 183.
14. Ibid., pp. 183–84.
15. Maurice Merleau-Ponty, *Signs,* trans. Richard C. McCleary (Evanston, Ill.: Northwestern University Press, 1964) p. 43.
16. Merleau-Ponty, *Phenomenology of Perception,* p. 184.

17. Ibid., p. 187.
18. Ibid., p. 188.
19. *Signs*, p. 39.
20. Ibid.
21. Ibid., p. 40.
22. Ibid., p. 43.
23. Ibid.
24. Ibid., pp. 45, 43.
25. Ibid., p. 46.
26. *Phenomenology of Perception*, p. 188.
27. *Signs*, p. 42.
28. *Phenomenology of Perception*, p. 195.
29. Maurice Merleau-Ponty, *The Visible and the Invisible*, trans. Alphonso Lingis (Evanston, Ill.: Northwestern University Press, 1968), p. 103.
30. Ibid., p. 102.
31. Ibid. Emphasis mine.
32. "The Primacy of Perception," pp. 42, 49.
33. *Phenomenology of Perception*, p. 197.
34. Ibid.
35. *The Visible and the Invisible*, p. 212.
36. Ibid. Emphasis mine.
37. Ibid., p. 102.
38. Ibid.
39. Ibid., p. 155. "In a sense the whole of philosophy, as Husserl says, consists in restoring a power to signify, a birth of meaning, or a wild meaning, an expression of experience by experience, which in particular clarifies the special domain of language. And in a sense, as Valery said, language is everything, since it is the very voice of the things, the waves, and the forests. And what we have to understand is that there is no dialectical reversal from one of these views to the other; we do not have to reassemble them into a synthesis: they are two aspects of the reversibility which is the ultimate truth."

3   Being in the Interrogative Mood

1. *The Visible and the Invisible*, trans. Alphonso Lingis (Evanston, Ill.: Northwestern University Press, 1968), p. 129.
2. Ibid., p. 235.
3. Ibid., p. 103.
4. Ibid., p. 102.
5. ". . . the problem then becomes one . . . of making explicit our primordial knowledge of the 'real,' of describing our perception of the world as that upon which our idea of truth is for ever based. We must not, therefore, wonder whether we really perceive a world, we must instead say: the world

is what we perceive." *Phenomenology of Perception,* trans. Colin Smith (New York: Humanities Press, 1962) , p. xvi.

6. *The Visible and the Invisible,* p. 41.

7. Ibid.

8. Ibid., p. 42.

9. David Hume, *An Inquiry concerning Human Understanding* (Indianapolis: Bobbs-Merrill, 1955) , p. 160.

10. Ibid., pp. 161–162.

11. *The Visible and the Invisible,* p. 8.

12. Ibid., p. 15.

13. Ibid., p. 6.

14. Ibid.

15. ". . . we must presuppose nothing—neither the naïve idea of being in itself, therefore, nor the correlative idea of a being of representation, of a being for consciousness, of a being for man: these, along with the being of the world, are all notions that we have to rethink with regard to our experience of the world." *The Visible and the Invisible,* p. 6.

16. Ibid., p. 103.

17. "From the point of view of *Being and Nothingness,* the openness upon being means that I visit it in itself; if it remains distant, this is because nothingness, the anonymous one in me that sees, pushes before itself a zone of void where being no longer only is, but *is seen.*" *The Visible and the Invisible,* p. 99.

18. Ibid., pp. 101–2.

19. *Phenomenology of Perception,* p. 343. Translation altered.

20. *The Visible and the Invisible,* p. 28.

21. *Phenomenology of Perception,* p. 342.

22. Ibid., pp. x–xi. Cf. *The Visible and the Invisible,* p. 239: "One does not get out of the rationalism-irrationalism dilemma as long as one thinks 'consciousness' and 'acts'—The decisive step is to recognize that in fact a consciousness is intentionality without acts, *fungierende,* that the 'objects' of consciousness themselves are not something positive *in front of* us, but nuclei of signification about which the transcendental life pivots, specified voids—"

23. The true is posited in "express acts which enable me to posit before myself an object at its distance, standing in a definite relation to other objects, and having specific characteristics which can be observed. . . ." *Phenomenology of Perception,* p. 343.

24. Ibid., p. x.

25. *The Visible and the Invisible,* p. 41.

26. Ibid., p. 3.

27. Ibid., p. 8.

28. Ibid. See also *Phenomenology of Perception,* p. 343.

29. *Phenomenology of Perception,* pp. 230–35; *The Visible and the Invisible,* pp. 7–8.

30. ". . . this indefatigable ranging over the things, which is our life, is

also a continual interrogation. It is not only philosophy, it is first the look that questions the things." *The Visible and the Invisible,* p. 103.

31. Ibid., p. 102. "If we are ourselves in question in the very unfolding of our life, it is not because a central non-being threatens to revoke our consent to being at each instant; it is because we are one sole continued question, a perpetual enterprise of taking our bearings on the constellations of the world, and of taking the bearings of the things on our dimensions." *The Visible and the Invisible,* p. 103.

32. Ibid., p. 121.

33. Ibid., p. 103.

34. Ibid., p. 129.

35. Ibid., p. 100.

36. Ibid., p. 77.

37. Ibid., p. 105.

38. Ibid., p. 100.

39. Ibid., p. 120.

40. "The visible can thus fill me and occupy me only because I who see it do not see it from the depths of nothingness, but from the midst of itself; I the seer am also visible. What makes the weight, the thickness, the flesh of each color, of each sound, of each tactile texture, of the present, and of the world is that he who grasps them feels himself emerge from them by a sort of coiling up or redoubling, fundamentally homogeneous with them; he feels that he is the sensible itself coming to itself. . . ." Ibid., pp. 113–14. In the constructive chapter "The Intertwining—the Chiasm" this becomes the central focus of Merleau-Ponty's revised phenomenology of perception—for, as he says, the principal fault of his *Phenomenology of Perception* was that it founded the analysis of perceptual experience on the concept of subjectivity, and not on the concept of implantation in the field of being. Cf. *The Visible and the Invisible,* pp. 183, 238–39.

41. Ibid., p. 103.

42. Ibid. "The decisive step is to recognize that . . . the 'objects' of consciousness themselves are not something positive *in front of* us, but nuclei of signification about which the transcendental life pivots, specified voids . . . the transcendent, the thing, the '*quale*' [having] become 'level' or dimension . . ." Ibid., pp. 238–39.

43. Ibid., p. 197.

44. Ibid. "With the first vision, the first contact, the first pleasure, there is initiation, that is, not the positing of a content, but the opening of a dimension that can never again be closed, the establishment of a level in terms of which every other experience will henceforth be situated." Ibid., p. 151. "The concept, the signification are the singular *dimensionalized,* the formulated structure, and there is no vision of this invisible hinge; nominalism is right: the significations are only *defined separations* (*écarts*) —" Ibid., pp. 237–38.

45. Ibid., p. 235.
46. Ibid., p. 103.
47. Ibid., p. 5.
48. Ibid., p. 136.
49. "Sartre et l'ultra-bolshévisme," in *Les aventures de la dialectique* (Paris: Gallimard, 1955), pp. 131–271.
50. *The Visible and the Invisible*, pp. 68, 236–37.
51. Ibid., p. 195.
52. Ibid., p. 193.
53. Ibid., pp. 204–6.
54. Ibid., p. 131.
55. Ibid., p. 132.
56. Ibid.
57. Ibid.
58. Ibid., p. 136.
59. Ibid., pp. 132, 192.
60. Ibid., p. 135.
61. Ibid., p. 214.
62. Ibid., p. 129.
63. Ibid., pp. 100–101.
64. Ibid., p. 125.
65. Ibid., p. 4.
66. Maurice Merleau-Ponty, *La prose du monde* (Paris: Gallimard, 1969).
67. *The Visible and the Invisible*, p. 15.
68. Ibid., p. 130.
69. Ibid., pp. 184–85, 225–26.

4 Merleau-Ponty and the Primacy of Reflection

1. Maurice Merleau-Ponty, *The Primacy of Perception and Other Essays,* ed. James M. Edie (Evanston, Ill.: Northwestern University Press, 1964), p. 19.
2. Ibid.
3. Maurice Merleau-Ponty, *Phenomenology of Perception,* trans. Colin Smith (New York: Humanities Press, 1962), p. 42.
4. L. Kolakowski, *The Alienation of Reason: A History of Positivist Thought,* trans. N. Guterman (Garden City, N.Y.: Doubleday Anchor, 1969).
5. *Phenomenology of Perception*, p. xv.
6. Ibid., p. 220.
7. Ibid., p. xvii.
8. Ibid., pp. 28 and 169. Also see pp. xiv, 23, 42–43, 63, 296, 347, and 446.
9. Ibid., p. 60.
10. Ibid., p. 324.

11. Ibid., p. 23.

12. Ibid., p. 229.

13. Ibid., p. 158.

14. Maurice Merleau-Ponty, *Signs,* trans. Richard C. McCleary (Evanston, Ill.: Northwestern University Press, 1964), p. 122.

15. Maurice Merleau-Ponty, *The Structure of Behavior,* trans. Alden L. Fisher (Boston: Beacon Press, 1963), p. 173.

16. *Phenomenology of Perception,* p. 109.

17. Ibid., pp. 146, 250, and 380.

18. *The Structure of Behavior,* p. 163.

19. Ibid., pp. 8–9.

20. Ibid., p. 9.

21. Ibid., pp. 43, 150, and 156–57.

22. Ibid., p. 150.

23. Ibid., pp. 29 and 43.

24. *Phenomenology of Perception,* p. 21.

25. Ibid., pp. 24 and 38–40.

26. Ibid., p. 28. Translation altered.

27. Ibid., pp. 26, 28, and 29.

28. Ibid., p. 23.

29. Ibid., p. 11.

30. Ibid., p. 30.

31. Ibid., p. 41.

32. Ibid., pp. 7 and 23–24.

33. *The Structure of Behavior,* p. 161.

34. *Phenomenology of Perception,* p. 119. See also p. 258.

35. Ibid., pp. xiv, 45, 61, 213, 219, 329, and 359.

36. Ibid., pp. 23 and 198–99.

37. J. L. Austin, *Philosophical Papers* (London: Oxford University Press, 1970), p. 57.

38. Ibid.

39. *Phenomenology of Perception,* pp. 58–59, 136 and 244.

40. R. M. Herbenick, "On Speaking of Experience: Merleau-Ponty's Conceptual Model," *The University of Dayton Review* 8, no. 1 (Summer 1971), 65–91.

41. *The Structure of Behavior,* p. 47.

42. *Phenomenology of Perception,* pp. 48–49.

43. Ibid., pp. vii, 57, 63, 206, and 219–20.

44. Ibid., pp. x and 63.

45. *The Structure of Behavior,* p. 213.

46. *Phenomenology of Perception,* pp. 164–65.

47. Ibid., p. 347.

48. Ibid., pp. xviii and 10.

49. Ibid., pp. xiv, 58–59, and 54.
50. Ibid., p. 256.
51. Ibid., p. vii.
52. Ibid., p. xviii.
53. Ibid., p. xix.
54. Ibid., pp. 84 and 365.
55. Ibid., pp. xviii, 157, 136, 232, and 351.
56. Ibid., p. 232.
57. Ibid., pp. 58–59.
58. *The Structure of Behavior,* p. 168.
59. *Phenomenology of Perception,* p. 160.
60. Ibid., p. 394; see also p. 127.
61. Ibid., p. 164.
62. P. F. Strawson, *Individuals* (Garden City, N.Y.: Doubleday Anchor, 1963), pp. 84–88.
63. *Phenomenology of Perception,* pp. 82, 84, 86, 101, 57, 140–41, 144, 130, 254, and 395.
64. Maurice Merleau-Ponty, *The Visible and the Invisible,* trans. Alphonso Lingis (Evanston, Ill.: Northwestern University Press, 1968), p. 101.
65. Ibid.
66. Ibid., p. 28.
67. Ibid., p. 130.
68. Ibid., p. 150.
69. Ibid., p. 157.
70. Ibid., p. 16. See also pp. 20, 23, and 26.
71. Ibid., p. 20.
72. Ibid., p. 14.
73. Ibid., pp. 29 and 38.
74. Ibid., p. 88.
75. Ibid., p. 46.
76. Ibid., p. 74. See also p. 85.
77. Ibid., p. 127.
78. Ibid., p. 97. See also p. 127.
79. Ibid., p. 125.
80. Ibid., p. 102.
81. Ibid., p. 140.
82. Ibid., p. 35.
83. Ibid.
84. Ibid., pp. 35–36.
85. Ibid., p. 38.
86. Ibid.
87. Ibid., p. 39.
88. Ibid., pp. 134 and 158.

89. Ibid., p. 167.
90. Ibid., pp. 7, 131–33, and 146.
91. Ibid., p. 32.
92. Ibid., pp. 147–48.
93. Ibid., p. 35.
94. Ibid., pp. 238–39.
95. Ibid., pp. 140, 148, and 160.
96. Ibid., p. 148.
97. *Phenomenology of Perception*, pp. 119, 121, 258, 281, 331, and 417.
98. *The Visible and the Invisible*, p. 156.
99. Ibid., pp. 156–57.
100. Ibid., p. 158.
101. Ibid.
102. Ibid., p. 159.
103. Ibid.
104. Ibid.
105. Ibid., p. 156. See the editor's footnote.
106. Ibid., pp. 110–11.
107. Ibid., p. 134.
108. Maurice Merleau-Ponty, *Themes from the Lectures*, trans. John O'Neill (Evanston, Ill.: Northwestern University Press, 1970), p. 11.
109. Maurice Merleau-Ponty, "Pages d' 'Introduction à la Prose du Monde,' " *Revue de Métaphysique et de Morale* 72, no. 2 (Avril–Juin 1967), 143.

5   The Question of Ontology

1. Jean-Paul Sartre, *Situations*, trans. Benita Eisler (New York: George Braziller, 1965), p. 227.
2. Maurice Merleau-Ponty, *The Visible and the Invisible*, trans. Alphonso Lingis (Evanston, Ill.: Northwestern University Press, 1968), p. 129.
3. Maurice Merleau-Ponty, *Phenomenology of Perception*, trans. Colin Smith (New York: Humanities Press, 1962), p. vii.
4. *The Visible and the Invisible*, p. 33.
5. Ibid., pp. 44–45.
6. Jean-Paul Sartre, *Situations I* (Paris: Gallimard, 1939), p. 34.
7. *The Visible and the Invisible*, p. 56.
8. *Phenomenology of Perception*, p. xi.
9. Ibid., p. xii.
10. *The Visible and the Invisible*, p. 58.
11. Ibid., p. 59.
12. Ibid., p. 62.
13. Ibid., p. 69.

14. Ibid., p. 85.
15. Ibid., p. 89.
16. Jean-Paul Sartre, *Being and Nothingness,* trans. Hazel E. Barnes (New York: Philosophical Library, 1956), p. L.
17. Ibid., p. 77.
18. Ibid., p. 78.
19. Ibid., p. lvii.
20. Ibid., p. lix.
21. Ibid., p. lxii.
22. Ibid., p. lxiii.
23. Ibid., p. lxvi.
24. Ibid.
25. *The Visible and the Invisible,* p. 68.
26. Ibid., p. 68.
27. *Phenomenology of Perception,* p. 4.
28. *The Visible and the Invisible,* p. 75.
29. Ibid., p. 123.
30. Ibid., pp. 130–31.
31. Ibid., p. 133.
32. Ibid., p. 137.
33. Ibid., pp. 137–38.
34. Ibid., pp. 147–48.
35. Ibid., p. 138.
36. Ibid., p. 139.
37. Ibid.
38. Ibid., p. 71.
39. Ibid., p. 83.
40. Ibid., p. 78.
41. Ibid., p. 77.
42. Ibid., p. 83.
43. Maurice Merleau-Ponty, *Les aventures de la dialectique* (Paris: Gallimard, 1955), pp. 131–271.
44. *Phenomenology of Perception,* p. 362.
45. Ibid.
46. Maurice Merleau-Ponty, "Western Marxism," *Telos,* No. 6 (1970), pp. 140–62.
47. *The Visible and the Invisible,* p. xxvi.

6   Merleau-Ponty's Conception of History

1. Maurice Merleau-Ponty, *Phenomenology of Perception,* trans. Colin Smith (New York: Humanities Press, 1962), pp. 431–32.

2. Ibid., p. 430.

3. Ibid., pp. 326–27.

4. Ibid., p. 406.

5. Ibid., p. 455.

6. Maurice Merleau-Ponty, *Themes from the Lectures,* trans. John O'Neill (Evanston, Ill.: Northwestern University Press, 1970), p. 41.

7. *Phenomenology of Perception,* p. 354.

8. Ibid., pp. 442–43.

9. Ibid., pp. 443–44.

10. Maurice Merleau-Ponty, *Les aventures de la dialectique* (Paris: Gallimard, 1955), p. 31–32.

11. Ibid., p. 32.

12. Ibid., p. 31.

13. Ibid.

14. *Themes from the Lectures,* p. 32.

15. Karl Marx and Freidrich Engels, *Selected Works in Two Volumes* (Moscow, n. d.), 1: 362–63 and 365; Maurice Merleau-Ponty, *Sense and Non-Sense,* trans. Hubert L. Dreyful and Patricia A. Dreyfus (Evanston, Ill.: Northwestern University Press, 1964), pp. 125–26 and 127.

16. *Sense and Non-Sense,* pp. 128–29.

17. *Phenomenology of Perception,* pp. 448–49.

18. Ibid., p. 447.

19. Ibid.

20. *Sense and Non-Sense,* p. 134.

21. Maurice Merleau-Ponty, *Humanism and Terror,* trans. John O'Neill (Boston: Beacon Press, 1969), p. 108.

22. Ibid., p. 130.

23. Ibid., p. 101.

24. Ibid., p. 124.

25. *Karl Marx: Early Writings,* trans. T. B. Bottomore (New York: McGraw-Hill, 1964), p. 58.

26. *Humanism and Terror,* p. 115.

27. Ibid.

28. Ibid., p. 116.

29. Ibid., pp. 116–17.

30. See, for example, Marx's extended treatment of this question in *The German Ideology,* trans. S. Ryazanskaya (Moscow, 1964).

31. *Les aventures de la dialectique,* p. 70.

32. Ibid., p. 89.

33. Ibid.

34. ". . . the structure of the relations of production determines the *places* and *functions* occupied and adopted by the agents of production, who are never anything more than the occupants of these places, insofar as they are the

'supports' (*Träger*) of these functions. The true 'subjects' (in the sense of constitutive subjects of the process) are therefore not these occupants or functionaries, are not, despite all appearances, the 'obviousnesses' of the 'given' of naïve anthropology, 'concrete individuals', 'real men'—but *the definition and distribution of these places and functions. The true 'subjects' are these definers and distributors: the relations of production."* Louis Althusser, Etienne Balibar, and Roger Establet, *Reading Capital,* trans. Ben Brewster (London, 1970), p. 180.

35. Maurice Merleau-Ponty, *Signs,* trans. Richard C. McCleary (Evanston, Ill.: Northwestern University Press, 1964), pp. 114–25.

36. "Action that will change the world is no longer undivided philosophical and technical praxis, that is to say an infrastructural movement and at the same time an appeal to a total critique of the subject, but rather a technical action comparable to that of an engineer constructing a bridge." *Les aventures de la dialectique,* p. 86. In commenting on Althusser's article, "Note sur le materialisme dialectique" in the *Revue de l'enseignement philosophique,* Oct.–Nov. 1953, p. 12, he says, "this mixture of dialectic and positivist spirit transports into nature the modes of being of man: it is nothing less than magic." Ibid., p. 87.

37. Ibid., pp. 116–17.

38. The lectures were given from 1952 to 1960. Short summaries can be found in the already cited work, *Themes from the Lectures.*

39. Ibid., p. 33.

40. Ibid., p. 34.

41. Ibid., p. 103.

42. Ibid., pp. 102–4.

7 Ambiguous Radicalism

1. Maurice Merleau-Ponty, *Sense and Non-Sense,* trans. Hubert L. Dreyfus and Patricia Allen Dreyfus (Evanston, Ill.: Northwestern University Press, 1964), p. 130.

2. Ibid., p. 131.

3. Maurice Merleau-Ponty, *Phenomenology of Perception,* trans. Colin Smith (New York: Humanities Press, 1962), p. 137.

4. Ibid., p. 172. Translation altered.

5. Maurice Merleau-Ponty, *Humanism and Terror,* trans. John O'Neill (Boston: Beacon Press, 1969), pp. 27–28. Translation altered.

6. *Sense and Non-Sense,* p. 46.

7. *Humanism and Terror,* p. 98. Translation altered.

8. Maurice Merleau-Ponty, *Themes from the Lectures,* trans. John O'Neill (Evanston, Ill.: Northwestern University Press, 1970), pp. 29–30.

9. Jean-Paul Sartre, "Merleau-Ponty," *Situations,* trans. Benita Eisler (New York: George Braziller, 1958), p. 322. Translation altered.

10. *Themes from the Lectures,* p. 33.

11. See Andrew Arato's contribution to *The Unknown Dimension: Post-Leninist Marxism,* ed. Dick Howard and Karl E. Klare (New York: Basic Books, 1972), and Paul Breines's Introduction to Lukács in *Telos,* No. 5, Spring 1970.

12. Maurice Merleau-Ponty, *Les aventures de la dialectique* (Paris: Gallimard, 1955), p. 279.

13. The French Communist party took Merleau-Ponty's political suggestions as a serious threat, as is witnessed by the public attacks on his book first presented at the Palais de la Mutualité in Paris, and then published as *The Misadventures of Anti-Marxism.* The PCF was no doubt right in seeing Merleau-Ponty's position as lending strength to the third force movement of Mendès-France and the group around the journal *L'Express,* for which Merleau-Ponty had been writing after leaving *Les Temps Modernes.*

14. *Les aventures,* p. 12.

15. Alfred Willener, *The Action Image of Society,* trans. A. M. Sheridan Smith (New York: Pantheon, 1971). Willener's book is a significant contribution to the style of political interrogation that, as I argue below, emerges as central to Merleau-Ponty's thought.

16. Maurice Merleau-Ponty, *Signs,* trans. Richard McCleary (Evanston, Ill.: Northwestern University Press, 1964), p. 71. Translation altered. See also Merleau Ponty's *La prose du monde* (Paris: Gallimard, 1969), p. 18.

17. *Les aventures,* p. 32.

18. Ibid., p. 44.

19. *Sense and Non-Sense,* p. 131.

20. *Phenomenology of Perception,* p. 398. Translation altered.

21. *Les aventures,* p. 117.

22. *Sense and Non-Sense,* p. 116.

23. *Les aventures,* p. 71.

24. Ibid., p. 192.

25. *Signs,* p. 280. Translation altered.

26. For a more political critique of Lenin and an alternative notion which is far more convincing, see *Selected Political Writings of Rosa Luxemburg,* ed. Dick Howard (New York: Monthly Review Press, 1971).

27. *Signs,* p. 280. Translation altered.

28. *Les aventures,* pp. 106–7.

29. Ibid., p. 72.

30. Ibid., p. 71.

31. *Sense and Non-Sense,* p. 116.

32. *Les aventures,* p. 112.

33. Lefort's important essay, "La contradiction de Trotsky," originally pub-

lished in *Les Temps Modernes,* has recently been reprinted in an interesting volume of his essays, *Eléments d'une critique de la bureaucratie* (Genève, Paris: Librairie Droz, 1971).

34. See Karl Marx, *Critique of Hegel's 'Philosophy of Right,'* ed. Joseph O'Mallay (London: Cambridge University Press, 1970) and, Dick Howard, *The Development of the Marxian Dialectic* (Carbondale: Southern Illinois University Press, 1972).

35. *Les aventures,* pp. 292–93.

36. Ibid., p. 79.

37. *Sense and Non-Sense,* p. 63.

38. *Les aventures,* pp. 47–78.

39. Maurice Merleau-Ponty, *The Visible and Invisible,* trans. Alphonso Lingis (Evanston, Ill.: Northwestern University Press, 1968), pp. 100–101.

40. *Phenomenology of Perception,* p. xx. Translation altered.

41. *Signs,* p. 311. Translation altered.

42. *Phenomenology of Perception,* p. 171. Translation altered.

43. *Les aventures,* p. 269.

44. On Sartre's *Critique de la raison dialectique,* see my critical exposition in *The New Marxism,* ed. Paul Piccone and Bart Grahl (St. Louis: New Critics Press, 1972).

45. *Les aventures,* p. 88.

46. *Sense and Non-Sense,* p. 94.

47. "Eye and Mind," in *The Primacy of Perception and Other Essays,* ed. James M. Edie (Evanston, Ill.: Northwestern University Press, 1968), p. 178.

48. *Signs,* p. 77. Translation altered. See also *La prose du monde,* pp. 125–26.

49. *La prose du monde,* p. 121.

50. Cf. Marx's own view: "We do not face the world in a doctrinaire fashion, declaring, 'Here is the truth, kneel here!' . . . We do not tell the world, 'Cease your struggles, they are stupid; we want to give you the true watchword of the struggle.' We merely show the world why it actually struggles; and consciousness is something that the world *must* acquire even if it does not want to." (Marx to Ruge, September, 1843.)

51. *The Visible and Invisible,* p. 137. Translation altered.

52. *Sense and Non-Sense,* p. 81.

53. *Phenomenology of Perception,* pp. 316–17.

54. *La prose du monde,* p. 121.

55. R. Garaudy et al., *Mésaventures de l'anti-Marxisme, Les malheurs de M. Merleau-Ponty* (Paris: Editions Sociales, 1956), p. 102.

56. *La prose du monde,* p. 160.

57. *The Visible and Invisible,* pp. 258–59.

58. *Humanism and Terror,* p. 179. Translation altered.

59. Ibid., p. 110. Translation altered.

60. J. Kanapa's polemic which, though hardly convincing, tries to make this point. *Mésaventures*, pp. 139–48.

8   Merleau-Ponty and Husserl

1. Edmund Husserl, *The Crisis of European Sciences and Transcendental Phenomenology*, trans. David Carr (Evanston, Ill.: Northwestern University Press, 1970).

2. Maurice Merleau-Ponty, *The Visible and the Invisible*, trans. Alphonso Lingis (Evanston, Ill.: Northwestern University Press, 1968).

3. "Philosophy as Rigorous Science," trans. Quentin Lauer, in Edmund Husserl, *Phenomenology and the Crisis of Philosophy*, ed. Quentin Lauer (New York: Harper Torchbooks, 1965), pp. 71–147.

4. On the origins of *The Crisis* studies, see the information given by Carr in the English translation and by the editor of the German critical text, Walter Biemel [Edmund Husserl, *Die Krisis der europäischen Wissenschaften und die transzendentale Phänomenologie*, ed. Walter Biemel, Husserliana vol. 6 (The Hague: Martinus Nijhoff, 1962). pp. xiiif.]

5. *The Crisis*, sec. 3, pp. 8–9.

6. Ibid., sec. 5, pp. 11–14.

7. Ibid., sec. 15, pp. 70–73.

8. Husserl, *Phenomenology and the Crisis of Philosophy*, sec. 38, p. 146.

9. *The Crisis*, sec. 56, p. 192.

10. Ibid., sec. 33, p. 121.

11. Ibid., sec. 12, p. 65.

12. Sec. 73, Husserliana edition; Appendix IV, Carr Translation.

13. Ibid., p. 336.

14. Ibid., sec. 5, p. 13.

15. Ibid., sec. 73, p. 339.

16. Ibid., sec. 36, p. 139.

17. A minimal sketch of elements involved is offered in my *Logos and Eidos: the Concept of Phenomenology*, Janua Linguarum, series minor, 93 (The Hague: Mouton, 1971); but it needs far more elaboration to be either demonstrative or complete.

18. *The Visible and the Invisible*, p. 35. Translation altered.

19. Ibid., p. 49.

20. Ibid., p. 127.

21. Ibid., p. 46.

22. And this is what Merleau-Ponty signalizes in *The Visible and the Invisible* by his insistence on "latent intentionality" (p. 173) or *"fungierende* intentionality" (p. 244) or "operating, functioning essence" (p. 118).

23. Ibid., p. 244.

24. This criticism is basically the same as that offered in Ludwig Landgrebe, "Husserl's Departure from Cartesianism," trans. R. O. Elveton, in *The Phenomenology of Husserl: Selected Critical Readings,* ed. R. O. Elveton (Chicago: Quadrangle Books, 1970), p. 294.

25. "Phenomenology and the Sciences of Man," trans. John Wild, in Maurice Merleau-Ponty, *The Primacy of Perception and Other Essays,* ed. James M. Edie (Evanston, Ill.: Northwestern University Press, 1964), pp. 43–95. This English translation is based on the French polycopied version, *Les sciences de l'homme et la phenomenologie, Les Cours de Sorbonne* (Paris: Centre de Documentation Universitaire, 1961), which represents only part of the whole course Merleau-Ponty delivered under this title. A complete version, though more concise and bearing the notice of approval by Merleau-Ponty himself, appears in *Bulletin de Psychologie,* no. 236, 18, 3–6 (November 1964), 141–70.

26. "It is also stated in a passage of the *Nachwort* added to the *Ideas* that 'philosophy is an idea.' Husserl used the word 'idea' here in the Kantian sense of a limiting concept to designate a thinking which we cannot properly think through, or totalize, which we envisage only on the horizon of our efforts as the limit of a certain number of thought operations which we are able to perform. 'It is an idea which is realizable only in the style of a relative, provisional validity, and in a historical process without end, but which, under certain conditions, is also effectively realizable.'" *The Primacy of Perception,* p. 51.

27. *Primacy of Perception,* pp. 53–54.

28. For example, *The Visible and the Invisible,* p. 110.

29. Ibid., p. 43.

30. Ibid., p. 46.

31. The second half of the essay in *The Visible and the Invisible* by the editor, Claude Lefort, draws our attention to this very effort on the part of Merleau-Ponty, pp. xx–xxxiii.

32. *The Visible and the Invisible,* pp. 121–22; 127–28.

33. Ibid., pp. 128–29.

34. "Husserl's Departure from Cartesianism," in *The Phenomenology of Husserl: Selected Critical Readings,* p. 294.

35. *The Crisis,* pp. 340–41; *Krisis,* Husserliana, vol. 6 p. 275; italics in the English translation mine.